The Development of Imagery in

Calderón's *Comedias*

The Development of Imagery in

Calderón's *Comedias*

by

William R. Blue

Spanish Literature Publications Company
York, South Carolina
1983

TABLE OF CONTENTS

Preface

Legend has it that Palas/Athene, the grey-eyed maiden, sprang fully clothed in golden mail, spear in hand, from the head of Zeus. If one reads many articles about Calderón's theater, the myth of Palas/Athene might well occur to the reader since the plays most often discussed are usually the best ones that the dramatist wrote, and the reader may assume that the plays sprang from the artist's pen as fully formed as was the goddess. Unfortunately one cannot speak of Calderón in terms of the aforementioned myth for he did not, with masterworks in hand, pass suddenly from nothingness to maturity. The process of growth and development is, to the contrary, laborious and sometimes long. The first play that Calderón wrote, Amor, honor y poder is considerably different from his last work, Hado y divisa de Leonido y Marfisa and even the most cursory glance at the two plays will make that clear. Nevertheless, a careful consideration of those plays will show that there are major similarities despite the many differences. How the playwright's style changes and develops from his earliest works to his last is the subject of this study. By focusing on the plays to be considered in chronological order and, within that order, by examining the role of imagery and other dramatic techniques, especially as they elucidate character, theme, structure, and poetic coherence, the developmental processes that lead from one play to another, from one period to another, can be observed.

I have examined primarily, though not exclusively, imagery[1] because I believe that images lie at the poetic heart of Calderón's plays. Obviously an analysis that centers on imagery, despite its centrality, can give only a partial view of the complexities of a drama. One could examine in detail stagecraft, diction, syntactic patterns, or a myriad of other topics with an eye toward the developmental process and, I believe, arrive at similar conclusions. Detaching for careful examination any one element naturally causes a certain distortion or a loss of the whole and so this study, while analyzing what many consider to be one, if not the most, important stylistic device used by Calderón, pretends to be only a step toward a fuller appreciation of the dramatist's artistry.

Though I have chosen to arrange my comments around the use of imagery, I have, at the same time, tried to vary my approach from play to play so as to demonstrate the heterogeneity within what is still a homogeneous corpus.

Imagery, just as theme, character, and the rest of the elements that make up a drama, can never be fully explicated outside of its context. "An image," as Wolfgang Clemens says, "viewed outside of its context is only half the image."[2] Thus dramatic imagery must be seen in relation to its position and function in the overall context of the play, that is, in terms of the particular situation in which it arises, in regard to what follows immediately and what precedes, and in relation to the character who uses it.

It is apparent that the study of imagery in relation to context,[3] then, is concerned with the kinds of situations and speeches in which imagery is quite likely to be used. Such an investigation is also concerned with how these elements relate to the drama as a whole: are they, for example, concerned with moments of crisis, with turning points, or epiphanies? Again, one should watch for possible changes in the imagery associated with a character during an entire play or for changes in the atmosphere of a work which may be embodied in the function of the images. Image distribution and frequency should be studied for what they show about structure and theme. One needs to determine whether Calderón uses particular types of images in one play or in one period as opposed to different or similar images in other plays and other periods. The relationship between verbal and visual images especially in the dramas of the playwright's more mature years must also be noted.

Drama must create a past, a present, and an implicit future towards which everything in the play must inevitably point.[4] Drama is also a more time-bound genre than either novel or poetry; in these genres -- and especially in epic poetry -- there may be occasion for some pause or digression. In a successful play, every element must contribute its share to the coherence and movement that are characteristic of the most expertly constructed theater. The audience must be quickly enmeshed in the situation, in the background and characterization, and in the implicit future, therefore, every element of a play's structure must appear, attain meaning, and project that meaning into the experience of the play. Each image, then, should form part of that complex web as must every other aspect of a successful drama.

Studying the imagery and other techniques in individual plays has proven quite fruitful. In this critical vein, there have been several outstanding studies of Calderón, but though they are certainly enlightening, they do not usually say how the imagery fits within the overall picture of Calderonian drama. On the other hand, image lists culled from a variety of Calderón's plays are intriguing as indicators of the breadth and depth of the playwright's literary background, but stripped of their context as they usually are in such studies, the lists tell us very little about how individual images work in the individual plays. Besides, the cataloguing method gives the illusion that all images are equal in aesthetic quality and meaning. A statistical method might well be used, but the fact that Calderón employed, say, fifteen animal images in one play and eight cave images in another would tell us little about the meaning of those images. Moreover, the statistical method could lead to false conclusions because the eight cave images might function more adequately and more powerfully in their context than the larger number of animal images.

My own approach has been to combine the above methods and to examine the images in the individual plays as well as to establish relationships among plays from the same and from different periods. As a part of this study, I have used a series of computer generated concordances of the plays which have helped me focus more carefully on the image patterns and on related syntactical items. The concordances, I should stress, are nothing more than tools that have provided me with data that would have been nearly impossible to compile without a computer. It remains the task of the critic to interpret this statistical material and then to apply the findings to the individual plays and to the whole corpus.

The division of Calderón's works into periods presents some problems, primarily because many of the plays have not been accurately dated.[5] I have limited this study, therefore, to works that can be reasonably well fixed in time. Most critics agree that 1650-51, when Calderón took holy orders, is a key year in his life, and is important in his dramatic production. If those two years are used as a dividing point, there remain a rather large number of plays dated between 1623 and 1649. I do not think that all of the works done between these years can be treated as a single group. Such a classification would have to include Calderón's first efforts as a dramatist (e.g., Amor, honor y poder, Nadie fíe su secreto, and Las tres justicias en una) as well as those from the ' 30s and '40s (e.g.,La vida es sueño, and El Alcalde de Zalamea). The differences that I have observed between those earlier plays and those of the later years have led me to choose (admittedly somewhat arbitrarily) 1629 as the terminus ad quem for what I will label the first period. I see the apprenticeship of the ' 20s culminating in the performance of three major works in 1629: El príncipe constante, La dama duende, and Casa con dos puertas. The period from 1630 to 1649 I call the middle period, and it includes most of his well-known and technically mature works. It follows that the final period, then, is 1650 to 1681, during which years the myth and court spectacle dramas are written and performed.

In a period of structuralist and poststructuralist approaches to literature, it may seem odd to some even to talk about images. Image study was one of the central concerns of New Criticism and the New Critics have come under attack, sometimes justifiably, sometimes not, for their perceived excesses. But if the newer modes of criticism have taught us that we cannot correctly view any work as a totally self-enclosed and self-referential construct, the newer modes, sometimes through their excesses, have emphasized the most important contribution New Criticism made to the study of literature. Before anything else, before relating the work to any other context, one must be a sensitive reader of the text. One must appreciate structure, themes, characterization and the techniques used to create those constituent elements, among them, imagery.

Just as Calderón could not have written his plays as he did without his predecessors, this study could not have been undertaken without the work of many critics who have strived to understand, appreciate, and communicate the complexities and beauties of Calderón's theater. My debt to their love of the Spanish dramatist's hard-won skill is immeasurable. The image of Pallas/Athene that I used at the beginning applies equally well to the critic as to the playwright.

Besides my debt to Calderonian critics, I would also like to thank my colleagues at the University of Kansas: John S. Brushwood, Andrew P. Debicki, Robert C. Spires, Jon Vincent, and George Woodyard who generously offered their understanding, aid, guidance, criticisms, and patience throughout this project. I offer my appreciation to Everett Hesse, Louis Pérez, Gerald Wade, and Bruce Wardropper for reading early versions of this study in 1977-78. I would like to thank my graduate students at

K.U. for their challenging questions about some of the ideas included in this study. I am grateful to Dean Robert Adams, Greg Wetzel, Lloyd Huff, Pam Dane, Nancy Kreighbaum, Jacky Christy and Paula Oliver for their aid with the computer. I am indebted to Vice Chancellor Frances Horowitz, to the General Research Fund, and to the Small Grants Fund of the University of Kansas for supporting this work.

Introduction to Part I

In the earliest plays that Calderón wrote (1623-1629) one
can find the central elements that will make up his mature style.
Not all of the techniques are as flawlessly employed as they will
be in later works, but they are usually effective and placed
where they will function efficiently. The major image patterns
are already visible: nature and the elements, light and dark, the
horse, the asp, the cosmic forces. The themes of honor, love,
appearance and reality, fate and fortune are also in evidence
from the very beginnings of his writing career. Similarly, the
roots of his stagecraft in the division of the stage, mirror
scenes, unexpected entrances and warnings, and the clever use of
props and costume are already apparent. Admittedly, in light of
the later plays, some of the early works seem primitive and
undeveloped but one must take care not to let   vision become
overclouded by reading the early plays only in light of the last
ones. Calderón, in 1623, is just beginning his career as a
dramatist and he has much to learn. Yet even in these apprentice
plays one can perceive the mark of the master.
     As already noted, Calderón's images are the ones that he
will use constantly throughout his career. And, though they are
not as well-developed as they will become, and though they are
not as profound in their meanings, they are, nonetheless,
consciously employed for the creation of certain effects and for
the communication of certain messages.
     The first quality that one can note about the imagery is
that Calderón attempts to suit the images to their environment.
At times those settings are of a physical and palpable nature, of
which Estela's description of the runaway horse in Amor, honor y
poder (1623) is a good example. She is in the countryside as she
looks up and sees "desde aquellas cumbres altas / un caballo se
despeña / con una mujer". [6] In terms of the surrounding nature
she describes his headlong plunge:

```
En el viento
apenas pone las plantas,
porque un volante que al sol
le vuelve otro sol de plata,
lleno del viento que deja,
le va sirviendo de alas...
que parece que a los cielos
tira la hierba que arranca... (59a)
```

At times the surroundings are sumptuous palaces as in Alvaro's speech in Saber del mal y del bien (1628) in which his perspective shifts from the elegant rooms to the equally refined garden:

```
Por aqueste corredor,
línea y eclíptica breve
de hermosos soles, que dan
a un ocaso mil orientes,
desde el cuarto de la Reina
bizarras las damas suelen
bajar a aquestos jardines,
Chipres, donde Venus duerme.  (227b)
```

But on other occasions, the atmosphere is more emotional than physical as in Alejandro's complaint in Nadie fíe su secreto (1623-24)

```
¡Oh dichoso el que puede
rendirse a la verdad de un desengaño,
dando, mas advertido,
a libres gustos cárceles de olvido! (108a)
```

In some plays in this early period, the external
surroundings and the interior emotions blend through the imagery.
That mixture enhances the speaker's concept of self, of nature,
of situation, and of life as in Fernando's magnificent and well-
known sonnet from El príncipe constante (1629):

Estas que fueron pompa y alegría,
despertando al albor de la mañana,
a la tarde serán lástima vana,
durmiendo en brazos de la noche fría.
Este matiz, que el cielo desafía,
iris listado de oro, nieve y grana,
será escarmiento de la vida humana:
¡tanto se emprende en término de un día!
A florecer las rosas madrugaron,
y para envejecerse florecieron:
cuna y sepulcro en un botón hallaron.
Tales los hombres sus fortunas vieron,
que en un día nacieron y expiraron;
que pasados los siglos, horas fueron. (266b-67a)

Fernando enters carrying the flowers that Fénix wanted in order
to alleviate her feelings of melancholy. Fernando compares the
effect of time on the flowers to similar effects on human beauty;
the link forged between the particular situation and the
universal truths espoused in the play is brought about through
the use of imagery. Fénix, who craves esthetic pleasures[7], is
horrified by his words. Fernando also relates the fate of Man,
"Tales los hombres sus fortunas vieron", by implication, to his
own fortunes so that the flowers become emblematic of both Fénix
and himself.

Toward the end of the first period though, imagery also
begins to underscore character change whereas in the earliest

plays, almost all of the characters speak the same language. It would be difficult in plays like Amor, honor y poder or in Judas Macabeo, to distinguish one character from another strictly on the basis of image use. But by the time of La dama duende, as we will show, one can more easily demonstrate the creation of individual characters who have quite well-developed attitudes and points of view, and one can see that character delineation in both the imagery they employ as well as in a more personalized diction. One of the aspects that will be examined in this context is the frequency or recurrence of images and of certain grammatical constructs that clarify character and the relationship of character to situation.

In the earliest plays, the type of image that stands out most clearly is the epic simile. The epic simile, briefly stated, consists of an example drawn from general human experience or from nature that is then applied, point by point, to the situation of the speaker or to that of the person addressed.[8] In Nadie fíe su secreto, Alejandro, responding to Arias' query about his "sudden" love for Ana, says:

> ¿Tú no sabes que en el mundo
> un átomo no se mueve
> sin particular precepto
> que rigen causas celestes?
> Lo que ayer se aborrecía,
> hoy con extremo se quiere:
> y hoy una cosa se adora,
> que mañana se aborrece.
> Todo vive en la mudanza;
> y así, Don Arias, sucede
> la disposición que tiene.
> Otras veces la había visto;
> pero que hoy estuve, advierte,

```
    menos ciego, o ella estaba
    más hermosa que otras veces.
    Yo he de servirla... (94a)
```

The epic simile is a lengthy comparison joined to the context by
an overt link, in this case, y and así. The "story quality" of
the simile in which Alejandro points to a general law behind his
"sudden" change in opinion about the loved one is certainly
illustrative but it is also relatively protracted. Throughout
the first period, there is a perceptible movement towards more
and more concision as we will illustrate in our discussion of
Saber del mal y del bien wherein the concepts of epic simile,
simile, and metaphor are more fully explored.

 Another feature of the imagery in the early plays is that
Calderón tends to accumulate or pile up images one on the other
and, though the individual images are related through similarity,
they lack the kind of development in context that we shall later
come to expect. In Amor, honor y poder, Teobaldo and the King
expound on love:

```
    La esperanza en el amor
    es un dorado veneno,
    puñal de hermosuras lleno,
    que hiere y mata en rigor:
    es en los dulces engaños
    edad de las fantasías...
    un martirio del deseo,
    y una imaginada gloria,
    verdugo de la memoria...
    ...yo creo
    que es, amando, la esperanza
    luz que de noche se ofrece... (70a)
```

The seven distinct images in the passage are joined through the ideas of love and suffering but there is little progression towards a climactic end in the list. Calderón seems to become more and more self-conscious about these iterative passages and, towards the end of the first period, appears to be trying to lessen their annoyance by calling attention to them as "devices." Diego, in Hombre pobre todo es trazas (1628), for example, says:

> Dejo aparte locuciones
> poéticas, aunque aquí
> pudiera decir que fue
> su cabello oro de Ofir,
> su frente campo de nieve,
> sus cejas sobre marfil
> línea de ébano...
> Nada desto digo, aunque
> todo lo puedo decir. (205a)

In the last works from this period, most of the lists of independent images have disappeared.

We may also observe the beginnings of the dualities that will be evident in Calderón's last works, though once again here, they are neither so omnipresent nor powerful as they will be. Still, in Saber del mal y del bien, the opposing fates of the two main characters are underscored by the use of dualities and, in El príncipe constante, the opposition of the two world views of the Christians and the Moors comes through strongly.

Likewise, ambiguity begins to come to the fore as one of Calderón's favorite techniques. In a play as early as Nadie fíe su secreto, there are scenes wherein characters speak to each other on two levels and the audience can appreciate the ironic distinction between what the characters say and what they mean (see 102a/b and 106a for examples). In later works like El médico de su honra, a more pervasive and powerful ambiguity becomes one of the major aspects in the play.

In general in the first plays there is a certain prolix quality about the images and about the speeches that will disappear in the later works. Speeches are introduced by words and phrases that signal them as lengthy narrations and, in the stories that follow, all of the details about the past, present, or future situations or about parallel circumstances from which lessons may be drawn are carefully detailed. In some of the images, there is even an intervening step between the image and its application as in the King's speech in Amcr, honor y poder:

> Cuando el sol sobre la nieve
> su rubio esplendor desata,
> hace una nube de plata
> que del monte al valle llueve:
> uno corre y otro bebe

The King continues by explaining the relationship between that image and the glass of water that Estela brincs him:

> y así, en efectos tan llanos,
> de tus ojos soberanos
> la luz en las manos dio,
> y ese cristal desato
> de la nieve de tus manos

And now he applies this to the present situation:

> Yo, a tu luz turbado y ciego,
> busco el agua, pero ya
> mal mi fuego templará,
> si está en el agua mi fuego.

> Abrásome; pero luego
> que el cristal hermoso pruebo,
> el agua a los ojos llevo;
> que en tan confusos enojos
> tienen sed labios y ojos. (62b)

In these early plays, Calderón is writing in a manner in which everything is said directly and clearly. If an image is used, it is explained and clarified for the public, either overtly, as in the above example, or by adding other parallel images to the first one. This fondness for clarification, description, and delineation is, however, useful and important to his development as a dramatist because his diction and imagery can flourish, expand, and become richer in color and depth. In the last plays of this early period we will thus find an increase in interrelated imagery in more condensed forms rather than the more diffuse images in the earliest plays. It is not that the discursive elements have disappeared in the works from 1628 and 1629, but rather, they become fewer in number as imagery begins to obey other directives. This process of evolution towards conciseness and organic unity, points to the plays of 1628 and 1629 as transition works leading from the early plays to the great plays of the second period.

Judas Macabeo

Judas Macabeo (1623) deals with the war between the Jews, led by Judas Macabeo, and the Syrians, led by Lisías. The action takes place within the framework of two battles in which the Hebrew forces finally defeat Lisías' armies and retake the holy city of Jerusalem. Played out against that epic background is a love intrigue that involves seven of the principal characters. As Valbuena Briones notes, the play "posee marcado dinamismo y una tendencia al espectáculo. (4b).

The principal image patterns emphasize the themes of war, love, and nature. The war images of Marte, Palas, muerte, sangre, confusión, and guerra are further underscored by the use of both visual and auditory devices. Not only do the characters appear on stage in armor, carrying swords and lances, but the battle scenes are vividly described and individual fights are also shown. Signaling this violent atmosphere are the sounds of war drums and trumpets, "Tocan cajas" (10a), "Salen al son de cajas destempladas Lisías y Soldados" (11a), "Salen Judas, Simeón, Jonatás, y Tolomeo, al son de cajas destempladas" (27a). As in later plays, these auditory effects are used to create atmosphere in an extraverbal sense as they function as signs to the audience that expand and strengthen the verbal imagery.

Along with the presentation of the war ambience through verbal, visual, and auditory signs, there is a very "physical" quality to the play. Emphasizing the palpable reality of war, brave actions, and the menace of death, are constant references to parts of the body and to violence. We feel the immediacy of the action and of the characters' participation through the use of such words as, brazos (19 occurrences), cuerpo (11), sangre (10), pies (9), manos (9), plantas (8), ojos (7),and pecho (5). And we can sense the physical aspects of war through the allied use of pena(s) (24), muerte (26), llanto (9), and cruel (7). As a final visual reminder of the horror of war, in the last scenes, Jonatás enters with "la cabeza de Lisías" (31b).

The microcosm reflects the macrocosm, as is the rule in most of Calderón's plays. War on earth causes or is reflected in chaos in the heavens (note the A to B correspondence in the following):

> Verás la ciudad fundada
> sobre un sangriento diluvio,
> o que, oprimida la tierra,
> parezca la sangre jugo.
> Los elementos verás
> mezclarse entre sí confusos,
> juntando en un breve caos
> tierra, sangre, viento y humo. (28a)

The four elements, classic images in all of Calderón's theater, are used to expand the situation of the individual and of the nation until all of the surrounding universe is drawn into the battle.

Of the nature images, the sun is the most used in this work. "Los rayos del sol" (5a) will crown Judas' head in a sign of joy and happiness as he returns victorious from the first battle. But this joyous moment gives way to common suffering as the death of Eleazaro is recounted, "Llore el sol / ... / Al sol que en temprano oriente / se corona de arreboles, / en términos del ocaso / pardas nubes se le oponen" (6b). The sun is also an image for Zarés who creates through her great beauty as much chaos and confusion on the personal level as does the war on a national level. Her tent, "del sol la esfera es" (23a) and, of course, men burn in the fire of their love (14b, 15b, 16b, 19a).

The love/war duality, an element in Calderón's theater that will appear many times, is manifest in this work. But even here, there is no simple split between love and war, but rather an intermingling of effects. At first, the sweet sounds of love serve as a respite from the horror of war:

> Y ahora con alegrarte
> quiero templar tu rigor,
> para ver si puede Amor
> suspender un poco a Marte (12a)

But out of these moments of peace, strife almost inevitably arises. From the love song that Lisías hears comes his instant passion for the yet unseen Zarés and from that grows Cloriquea's jealousy. Earlier, after Judas brusquely rejected Zarés' offer of love, to convince him of her self-sacrificing passion she decides to enter the war arena:

> Yo, Judas, para obligarte,
> pues en las armas te empleas,
> pues solo guerras deseas,
> pues solo te agrada Marte,
> en todo pienso imitarte,
> casta Palas he de ser (9a)

Love and war, love in war, and war in love are all dealt with effectively in this early play. The macrocosm and microcosm of the work are once more persuasively joined through the love imagery as the characters strive to win at love through winning at war.

Lest we overstate the case, though there are many elements in the play that are dramatically well presented, the work is not unblemished. The characters in the play are almost all cut from the same cloth. It is difficult, for example, on the basis of individualized imagery or diction, to tell them apart. Judas seems to stand out from all of the other characters in the play since he acts almost totally on his own. Yet he decides to enter the enemy camp and to kidnap Cloriquea only to show up Lisías. Lisías, on the other hand, is more emotionally understandable since he is drawn to the Hebrew camp because of a deeply felt passion. In addition, Cloriquea's instant conversion to Judaism in the final scene is hard to justify since just moments before she had called the Jews:

> cobardes hebreos,
> abatida sucesión
> de la más humilde sangre
> que Palestina crió,
> Infames samaritanas,
> pues la descendencia sois
> de aquel peregrino pueblo
> que Egipto tuvo en prisión (32a)

In character's speeches, moreover, we find little tonal modulation as can be shown if we compare a love speech with a war speech. Simeón singing the praises of his brother says:

> Cesa, valeroso hebreo,
> para cuyo eterno nombre
> es de la divina fama
> mudo el labio, sordo el bronce,
> cesa de dar alabanzas
> a mi honor con dulces voces;
> porque ante las glorias tuyas
> son ningunos mis blasones (6a)

and when he tells Zarés of his affection, the same oratorical tone predominates:

> Si los presentes trofeos,
> si las merecidas glorias

de conseguir las victorias,
de pretendidos empleos,
iguales en mis deseos,
y todos, bella Zarés,
se redujeran después
al imperio de mis manos,
más dichosos, más ufanos
salieran luego a tus pies (8a)

Accentuating this unmodulated presentation of character is the formal construction of the entire play. Not only do characters not develop naturally, but also their speeches have an "isolated" quality about them. Valbuena Bricnes notes that the speeches with which the play opens, those that tell us about the past history of the conflict between the Jews and the Syrians, appear "a modo de 'prólogo'" (3a). Most of the longer speeches, in fact, follow a set pattern in that they have a brief introduction, a lengthy narrative middle, and a brief conclusion wherein some action is promised. These speeches are generally set apart from the surrounding dialogue through the use of such phrases as, "Escucha y sabráslo" (5b), "estáme atento" (13a), "pues escucha y las sabrás" (13a), 'Aun no he dicho a lo que vengo" (13b), "escucha y dirélo en breve" (16a), "Escucha: / que yo es justo que lo diga" (18a); or by directly addressing the person to whom the speech is oriented, "Cesa, valeroso hebreo" (6a), "Vencedor divino y fuerte" (7b). "Yo, Zarés, que siempre he sido..." (8a), "Valiente Macabeo" (10a), "La fama de tu hermosura, / divina Zarés..." (16a). The division into neat sections of the speeches that supposedly flow emotionally from the heart is not particularly convincing. This formalism, nonetheless, does emphasize the epic quality of the play and, therefore, is partially functional.

Style in general is quite formal in the work. There are a number of rhetorical questions posed by many of the main characters; many passages of anaphora are scattered throughout the play; and in the images also we can note a rhetorical mode. In almost all passages involving imagery, there is a "principle of addition"[9] at work throughout the play, that is to say that elements are linked by the conjunction "y" more often than they are more smoothly and carefully integrated into the flow of the work. Judas will be the "castigo y venganza" of the Syrians (5a); he is characterized by "prudencia y valor" (5a); Simeón feels "pena y fuego", but persists in his love despite the rejection, "el desprecio y el amor" (8a); Jonatás, face to face with Zarés, feels "humilde y desconfiado", but will still "sufrir y padecer" in his love for the maiden; Zarés dons warrior's garb in order to "sujetar y vencer" Judas (9a); Judas promises a war in which he calls for his soldiers to "vengad el cielo y ofended la tierra" (10b); Lisías characterizes the Macabeos as "arrogantes y vanos" (11b); Jonatás tells Lisías that Jerusalem contains "el alcázar de David/ y de Salomón el templo" (13a); Zarés asks for arms with which to fight, "Dame el escudo y la espada" to which Chato immediately responds, "Espada y escudo tienes" (15a); Jonatás tells his brother not to intervene in his fight with Lisías until it is over and admonishes him, "oye y calla, advierte y mira" (21b). In many of these phrases, the second element is a repetition of the first rather than a development of an idea or of an image. Of course, this is not to say that Calderón does not use simple conjunctions to link elements in later works, but rather that the frequent use of the link and the repetitive quality of the phrases are not so common in later plays. Instead, Calderón will strive to balance opposites in his last works or to establish a central or even a local image and then to surround it with interrelated images in order to create a far more complex system of relationships among his descriptive phrases and images (see, for example, the balancing of opposite motifs in the later discussion of Eco y Narciso).

Later in his career, Calderón uses lists of images that serve to develop a feeling or an idea. For example, in La vida es sueño, Segismundo compares himself to "ave, bruto, pez y arroyo" and thereby brings in the four elements of nature and their representatives to universalize his comparison and to augment his sense of suffering and his lack of liberty. In Judas Macabeo, however, Jonatás employs a list of images when telling his father how Eleazaro died. Describing the elephant that crushed his brother, Jonatás says that the animal, like a:

>   bárbara losa le oprime,
>   rústica tumba le acoge,
>   bruta pira le fatiga
>   y urna funesta le esconde (7a)

The last three images and the verbs that are associated with them are simple repetitions of the first, used to create emphasis rather than to develop meaning. Despite the parallelism of the lines, the images are isolated elements -- also note that they are separated from each other by commas -- relatively independent of one another and of the pattern in which they are placed. Their independence can be shown by the fact that they could be shifted without any subsequent loss of sense or of power:

>   bruta pira le fatiga,
>   bárbara losa le oprime,
>   urna funesta le esconde
>   y rústica tumba le acoge

Such changes in the order of image patterns in passages in later plays could not be made without a consequent dissipation of force, order, and meaning. In a passage from El médico de su honra, for example, Gutierre lists a series of affronts:

        Esta noche iré a mi casa,
        de secreto entraré en ella
        por ver qué malicia tiene
        el mal: y hasta apurar ésta,
        disimularé, si puedo
        esta desdicha, esta pena,
        este rigor, esta ofensa,
        este asombro, este delirio,
        este cuidado, esta afrenta,
        estos celos...¿Celos dije?
        ¡Qué mal hice! Vuelva, vuelva
        al pecho la voz... (335a)

The development from "esta desdicha" to "esta afrenta / estos celos" is in an ever ascending order of meaning, feeling, and intensity. The list in El médico is cumulative, building in force to establish Gutierre's germinating confirmation of his most feared and unspoken doubts. From there, the next passage builds on the former toward the conception of the central image of the play. In Judas Macabeo, once again, the images are isolated and individually climactic.

To point to one final contrast between the imagery of this early play and that of later works, we can look at a passage that deals with nature imagery. Jonatás speaks to the night:

        Noche, si de mis suspiros
        estás obligada, ten
        tu curso, quítale al día
        de su beldad el poder;
        no obedezcas a la luz
        del sol, y, a mi amor fiel
        sepulta en oscuridad
        su dorado rosicler (23b)

Night accompanies Jonatás in his efforts to seduce Zarés and in this passage he makes it his accomplice. The image is a momentary or local one that does not have any profound resonance in the rest of the play and the passage is in the form of an apostrophe. Let us then compare Calderón's use of the night image in El médico. There, Gutierre associates himself with night and with darkness in a much more thorough way. The image of night becomes a central image in the work and a host of related imagery hovers about it. In the passages where the night image is used, there is in El médico a concision and a preciseness that is not to be found in the earlier play. It takes Calderón eight lines in the later play to create the image and to show its relationship with the main character. The effect is greater though the space taken up by the image is the same as in the former play:

> En el mudo silencio
> de la noche, que adoro y reverencio,
> por sombra aborrecida,
> como sepulcro de la humana vida
> de secreto he venido
> hasta mi casa... (336b)

In the later plays, Calderón is thinking more in patterns than in the creation of individual images hence he is more direct and more subtle at the same time.

In Judas Macabeo, to summarize, there are the beginnings of the devices and techniques that Calderón will use throughout his career as a dramatist. In the early plays, he seems to be more the poet than the dramatist and thus his images function better in the individual passage than in the overall drama . Characters and images seem isolated as do some of the speeches. His understanding of the uses of ambiguity and smooth transition is only beginning and is not as well-developed as it will later be.

Nevertheless, in this early play we can see and appreciate a grandeur of design, of theme, and of concept.

La gran Cenobia

Like Judas Macabeo, La gran Cenobia (1625) deals with great
issues: the fate of nations, the fate and fortunes of Emperors,
generals, and queens, as well as the themes of war, honor, and
love. Battles are fought, prophecies are declared, people are
condemned to death, noble men and women are humiliated, and a
brutal man rises momentarily to power. Once more, there is an
attempt to capture a sense of grandeur and a breadth of scope in
this semihistorical play. The characters are undoubtedly more
interesting and more convincingly portrayed here than in the
earlier work. We see and appreciate the stoic sufferings of
Astrea, Decio, and Cenobia and we can contrast their dignity with
the cowardice and harshness of Aureliano and Libio. Characters
are not all cut from the same cloth.

Some of Calderón's favorite techniques and devices are
evident in this work: prophecy, omens, unexpected voices, mirror
scenes, ambiguity, and many of his favorite themes appear too:
fortune, war, honor, and love. The ties between the techniques
and the themes are natural ones, in that, for example, the theme
of fortune seems to call for mirror scenes whereby the dramatist
may contrast a man's good then bad fortune or wherein one man's
rise can be opposed to another's fall.[10] In La gran Cenobia, for
example, Aureliano first humiliates Decio (74-75); then Decio
save Aureliano's life (86) only to be humiliated again (95a); and
finally Decio kills Aureliano and is subsequently named Emperor
(100-101).

But mirror scenes in this play also serve to compare
characters in more than this fashion. Cenobia's just, humble,
and noble treatment of the petitioning soldiers (77b) in Act I
may be later compared and contrasted with Aureliano's vaunting
pride before his petitioners.

In the treatment of fortune, the closely allied themes of
love, war, and honor find easy entry. The love-war, love-in-war,
war-in-love theme can once again be seen in this play. Here,
Decio falls in love with the beautiful woman-warrior, Cenobia.

Though they both desire Aureliano's death, Decio is compelled to
protect Rome's interests and, thus, while he loves Cenobia, he
must oppose her.   She feels drawn to him too on the personal
level, but her own national interests prevent her from openly
expressing her feelings. Their relationship is, then, based on
dualities love-honor,   love-duty,   personal-national.   Decio
declares his inner torment thus:

> en qué confusión tan fuerte
> me ponen amor y honor (87a)

 The dualities here differ from those in Eco y Narciso and in
other late plays because they are not so pervasive in this early
play as they will later become. Yet their use is nonetheless
effective because it presents the audience with what at first is
a seemingly unresolvable problem. The answer to that problem is
central to other questions that arise in the play: eliminate
Aureliano and then have Decio marry Cenobia. By this easy
solution, tyranny is expunged, a noble, loving man is married to
an equally noble and desirable woman, the war is ended, and order
is restored on both the macro and microcosmic planes.   In later
plays, the resolution is not so obvious and does not inevitably
lead to universal happiness, though a sense of order   is
preserved.

     In Judas Macabeo, many times a single image was not felt to
be sufficient to convey the strength of a character's emotion.
In La gran Cenobia, there are fewer cases of the kind of image
aggregation apparent earlier and now there is more emphasis on
the single but powerful image to carry the burden. Decio
accentuates the strength of his honor and of his arm saying:

> tal fuego el honor enciende
> que es un rayo cada golpe (87a)

Libio describes the cloak of darkness that will hide his treachery as:

las tinieblas del silencio ciego (89b)

But besides the single image, image lists are to be found in this play as well; in an image list, once more, subsequent images are repetitions of the first:

Sale al alba coronada
de rayos, y el sol despliega
al mundo cendales de oro,
que enjugan llanto de perlas.
Sube hasta el cenit; mas luego
declina, y la noche negra
por las exequias del sol,
doseles de luto cuelga.
Impelida de los vientos,
con alas de lino vuela
alta nave, presumiendo
todo el mar pequeña esfera;
y en un punto, en un instante,
brama el viento, el mar se altera,
que parece que sus ondas
van a apagar las estrellas.
El día teme la noche,
la serenidad espera
la borrasca, el gusto vive
a espaldas de la tristeza. (94a)

The two images, the first of the shining sun that is slowly overtaken by the dark and deadly night, and the second of the ship, at first on a calm sea but later tossed about by a wild storm, are summarized by yet a third, aphoristic image, "el gusto vive / a espaldas de la tristeza." There is a discursive quality to these images and, though they do emphasize a thematic concern, they are lengthy and spun out (see also 89b-90a, 73a, 80b for other examples).

· Calderón uses certain visual signs and props in the play to add to the unity of the work, for example, the banda that Cenobia gives Decio appears on 82a, 86b, 87a and the bastón given by Aureliano to Decio on 87a and 94b. These props help some characters recognize others while, often, they also help to disguise identities. Props and their manipulation will be of key importance in later works and the playwright has already recognized their usefulness here.

In a similar way, unexpected answers to questions or unforseen warnings, like the gunshots in El pintor de su deshonra, are used in this early work. When Astrea is cast into a ravine, her complaints addressed to her malefactor, Aureliano, are overheard by others who interpret them according to their own points of view. Cenobia hearing, "Hoy ha de triunfar de ti / el rigor" is sure that her cause is lost; Libio believes himself advised to be "soberbio, ... tirano/ ... riguroso, ... fiero" (85b); and Decio is called "emperador" by the voice. The difference between the use of such a device here and that used in later works like El pintor de su deshonra, El monstruo de los jardines, and La hija del aire is that there, the device is employed at several key moments through the play. In La gran Cenobia, however, the three characters, Cenobia, Libio, and Decio, file on stage one immediately after the other to hear the sibyline voice speak their future. A similar scene is not repeated in the play and this "one shot" parade of characters tends to lessen the dramatic effect.

Calderón has also seen that ambiguity can be most effective as a tool. Later, in El médico de su honra, Gutierre is able to upbraid Enrique by speaking on two levels just as Enrique, earlier in the play, deceived Gutierre by talking ambiguously about his "amigo." In the present play, Cenobia is the person

who most effectively uses two levels of meaning in her speeches.
Libio tries to disguise his hatred of his aunt, Cenobia, by
pretending to tell her "lo que todos van diciendo" (77b), but
Cenobia sees through his pretense to the core of his treacherous
soul, "¡Qué ciegamente ha mostrado / su intento!" (78b).
Cenobia later wants to warn her nephew that she is aware of his
machinations, so she pretends to read parts of a book she is
writing in the hopes that with this ruse he will understand her
message and desist from his unwise actions (83a). She then
turns to Libio and declares, "dijera entonces a él / lo que
ahora digo a ti" (83b). Ambiguity, seen here in the simple
example of a character pretending to talk to a nonexistent reader
but in reality directing her remarks to a specific listener, two
levels of language, and other efforts at polysemy will grow in
complexity and import in the later plays.

The seeds of Calderón's style were planted in the earliest
plays like Amor, honor y poder and Judas Macabeo and have grown
in La gran Cenobia. The dramas of his mature period are yet to
come and in the meantime, other techniques need to be closely
scrutinized and polished by the dramatist. Yet even here there
is a strong drive towards dramatic unity and towards an effort at
making each element contribute its part to the total effect of
the play. Those aspects that will make Calderón's style
recognizable as uniquely his are already in evidence in the plays
he was writing at only twenty five years of age. There are
dualities, mirror scenes, the integration of props, certain image
patterns that, for example, emphasize the relationship between
the personal and the cosmic situation:

> Rompan los vientos
> las voces siempre inquietas
> de las cajas y trompetas...
> Suene el clarín animado,
> gima el parche castigado,

> brame el bronce repetido.
> Publiquen sangrienta guerra,
> con mortales sentimientos,
> turbados los elementos
> agua, fuego, viento y tierra (84a)

There are also prophecies, warnings, and the major themes of fortune, love, and honor all make their appearance, in as of yet a youthful manner, in La gran Cenobia.

Saber del mal y del bien

The fact that differences in stylistic and structural
control exist should not lead to the conclusion that in a
particular play youthful exuberance becomes mature control and
that from that moment on, all of the works are finished
masterpieces. Such is not the case in a developmental process,
for there are many shifts and interrelations in the works
themselves that preclude absolute divisions.

There is, nevertheless, a recognizable difference between
Judas Macabeo (1623) and Saber del mal y del bien (1628) that can
be seen in the focus, imagery, dramatic unity, tonal control, and
structure of the two plays, yet there are also many similarities
between the later work and the earlier. The relationship between
plot and subplot in Saber is similar to that in Judas Macabeo.
In Judas Macabeo, the main action centers on a nation at war and
on the honor contest among several men while the secondary plot,
a love intrigue, involves seven of the principal characters. In
Saber, the main action also occurs on the national level and
there is a secondary love plot involving some of the principal
players. In this play, however, the main action is more focused
on the rising and falling fortunes of two noblemen rather than on
the fate of an entire nation, and the love plot involves only
four of the play's main characters.

In Saber, Don Alvaro de Viseo, a Portuguese noble fallen on
hard times, is rescued by Conde Pedro and placed in a position of
great importance by the Castilian King, Don Alfonso. During the
play, Pedro falls from favor as a result of the jealousy and envy
of two other noblemen and Alvaro, whose star is rising, attempts
to help his newfound friend. At the end of the play, both Alvaro
and Pedro find grace with the King and the two treacherous nobles
are chastened, then pardoned by Pedro. In the subplot, Hipólita,
Pedro's sister, and Laura, her friend, vie for Alvaro's love
while, at the same time, the King tries to win Hipólita's favor.

The play ends with two marriages, Alvaro to Hipólita and Pedro to Laura.

From the outset of Saber we recognize more tonal modulation than we saw in Judas Macabeo. There is a distinct difference, for example, between the language and tone of the love speeches and of those concerned with honor or with the fortunes of Pedro and Alvaro. In the love scenes, the characters generally speak either in the language of the logical love debate (228a/b, 230-31) or in courtly love terms, as befits the atmosphere of the play:

> Yo así, que siempre adoré
> rigores tuyos; yo así
> que tus desprecios sentí
> y tus desdenes amé,
> con veneno me crié;
> y estoy de gloria tan lleno
> cuando siento, lloro y peno
> tu desdén y tu rigor,
> que adoleciera mi amor
> a faltarle este veneno (217a)

The political scenes or those that treat the theme of fortune, on the other hand, are characterized by more serious, even "cosmic," tone and diction:

> El mundo todo es presagios,
> el Cielo todo es avisos,
> el tiempo todo mudanzas,
> y la fortuna prodigios (234a)

> Si no está culpado el Conde,
> él vencerá las sospechas,
> negras nubes que se oponen

a la luz de la nobleza;
como el sol, que desvelando
el horror de las tinieblas,
sale más puro... (240a)

There is also a turn, in <u>Saber</u>, towards more effective use
of such devices as the aside. Asides in this play are utilized
by characters to express surprise or to comment insightfully on
their situations and, therefore, to intensify characterization
and theme by creating a stronger sense of unity. In <u>Judas
Macabeo</u>, on the other hand, the aside served more to separate
characters from the action and from each other than to contribute
to a sense of cohesion. In Act III, of <u>Saber</u>, Alvaro comments in
an aside on the inconstancy of fortune, a central theme in this
work, and on his longing for peace and quiet. His speech is
similar to Luis de León's "Vida retirada": "¡Oh inconstancia
desigual... / déjame en aqueste estado, / ni envidiado ni
envidioso..." (236b). At the same time, he reminds us of the
action going on about him in this particular moment thus the
atmosphere of the play and its general theme are linked to the
particular moment through asides.

As the asides frequently link scenes and provide spatial
relationships for the audience, so also do more adroit
transitions from one scene to the next help to make the action
flow and and the scenes blend more smoothly than before.
Transitions from one scene to the next are handled in various
ways: one character may overhear the conversations of other
characters (219a); characters see another approaching and begin
to talk about the oncoming person, but the new arrival does not
overhear the conversation (220a); or key words mentioned at the
end of one speech are repeated by a new arrival. Perhaps the
best example of the last method occurs in Act III. The King
tells Alvaro that he has come to the mountains feigning a hunting
expedition, but his real motive is to see Hipólita, "Yo vengo a

caza por verla" (236a). He asks Alvaro, who also loves
Hipólita, to intercede with her on his (the King's) behalf.
Alvaro decries his bad luck and asks Fortune to stop her constant
turnings, "solo una cosa te pido, / Fortuna; y es... / déjame en
aqueste estado" (236b). At this moment, Pedro, fallen from the
King's graces, enters unexpectedly. He tells his servant that he
is searching for Alvaro to ask his help. He knows that Alvaro
must be near since he is accompanying the King, "que a caza
salió" (236b). He laments his bad fortune saying, "¿Estos son,
diosa Fortuna, / los efectos de tu rueda?" His speech, linking
as it does references from the King's earlier remarks (la caza)
with those of Alvaro in his short monologue (fortuna), ties the
speeches together but with a slightly modified viewpoint since
Pedro cannot know what the others do. He is speaking about his
own situation and about his own point of view but he does so
with the same words that the other characters used. Though
modified in meaning, this repetition of key words tightens the
structure of the play because characters do not exist in
isolation from each other nor in isolation from the reigning
atmosphere or tone of the play.

Besides verbally linking his scenes, Calderón utilizes the
repeated or mirror scene to give a stronger sense of unity to the
play. Many of the scenes and speeches that include Alvaro and
Pedro are mirror images of each other and this is not surprising
given the story line of the rising and falling fortunes of the
two men (compare the early scenes of the play with pp. 236-37 of
Act III).

As structural unity is tighter here, so also characters are
more fully developed than in Judas Macabeo All of the major
characters undergo changes in the course of the action. We can
see the transformations most obviously in Pedro and Alvaro, but
in the female characters too there is development. Jealousy and
love, for example, are not the only motives behind Hipólita's
actions. She also demonstrates her loyalty to the King (216-17);

her high concept of personal and family honor (239-40); her
ability to participate in clever repartee (228-29); and her
knowledge of her own limitations (see the pact made with Licia,
228a). Even the King seems to have grown by the end of the play
since at first he appeared to be a rash and impetuous man (218-
219), but he too demonstrates the ability to learn from his
experiences (233a, 235b, 242a).

Another development in Calderón's use of character involves
the grazioso figure. In Judas Macabeo, Chato, the gracioso, is a
peripheral character who provides little more than fleeting
moments of comic relief. García, the gracioso in Saber,
reflects the rising and falling fortunes of his masters. When he
attempts to change his luck by lying to the King in Act I, or
when he changes masters in hopes of bettering his lot in Act II,
he inevitably fails. He admits his errors and summarizes some of
the principal ideas about fortune when he says "¡Qué en vano /
sus estados muda el hombre! / Que el que fuere desdichado, / no
estará de su fortuna / seguro en ningún estado" (232a). The
gracioso's role is becoming larger and is mirroring the central
concerns of the play.

Calderón's growing mastery of the dramatist's skills can
also be seen in his treatment of the opening and closing scenes
of Saber. The initial action of Judas Macabeo, was delayed by a
lengthy prologue; in Saber, the audience is thrust immediately
into important events since the play begins with the conversation
between Hipólita and her friends, Laura and Jacinta. She talks
about the relationship between herself and the King and this
conversation is followed or better yet, interrupted by the
precipitous arrival of Alvaro and by the introduction to his
problems. The resolution of Saber is, however, less satisfactory
than its beginning. While more smooth and better prepared for
than the resolution of Judas Macabeo, the closing scene in Saber
is yet somewhat forced. The King's test of Iñigo and Ordoño is
rather unsophisticated. He decides to act after seeing that

Pedro is innocent and after remembering a lesson learned from his readings:

> Yo leí
> un discurso que decía
> que ningún hombre podía
> oír su culpa tan en sí,
> que no se turbase; y quiero
> con esta curiosidad
> acrisolar la verdad
> del desengaño que espero. (242a/b)

This seems ready-made. Furthermore, the marriage between Pedro and Laura is totally unexpected as there was never any hint of feelings between these two characters. It is at best a marriage of dramatic convenience.

We can also note changes in the poetic language between Judas Macabeo and Saber. In the earlier play, the principle of addition was the mark of most of the characters' language. In Saber, the simple but usually extended comparison is the norm. When the King wishes to express his surprise at Hipólita's favorable response to his presence, he states, using a comparison, that he misses her rigor:

> Un hombre, que se criaba
> con veneno, adolecía
> de un grave dolor el día
> que el veneno le faltaba.
> Yo así, que siempre adoré
> rigores tuyos; yo así
> que tus desprecios sentí
> y tus desdenes amé,
> con veneno me crié;
> y estoy de gloria tan lleno

> cuando siento, lloro y pero
> tu desdén y tu rigor,
> que adoleciera mi amor
> a faltarle este veneno. (217a)

Sometimes, this device is translated into even longer stories from which analogies are derived, as, for example, in Alvaro's story of Tebando and Alejandro (221b-22a) which he then applies to his own situation, "fácil es la aplicación." (see also 217a, 219b, 221/b, 225b, 228a). This type of lengthy comparison is traditionally known as an epic simile. An epic simile, "involves the comparison of one composite action or relation with another composite action or relation."[11] Usually the poet tries to provide one common denominator on which to base the comparison. A noted feature of this type of simile is its "digressive tendency" and a modified version of the simile is this "example -- application" form.

In the simile, there is a separation between tenor and vehicle. Tenor is the idea being expressed and the vehicle is the figure that carries the weight of the comparison. Hipólita sees Alvaro approaching and has a split reaction, "(Y parece que mi pecho / lo desea y lo aborrece)" (227a). She likens this reaction to the moth by means of a simile. "bien como la mariposa, / que se acobarda y se atreve / ...a la llama" (228a).

Since drama is a time-limited genre, a hierarchical system of poetic figures may be posited (though, I should add, this system is not absolute): comparison, simile, metaphor. The comparison would be the least economical way to draw two seemingly disparate but "poetically" similar elements together: A is like B for the following reasons; or, here is an example, A, that may be compared to the specific situation, B. In the simile there is, on the one hand, more economy, but on the other, the link is still specifically announced: A is *like* B, but no reasons are necessary. In metaphor, tenor and vehicle are still recognized as separate, but they are drawn into a "tensive" relationship.[12] Metaphor is "a condensed verbal relation in which an idea, image, or symbol may, by the presence of one or more other ideas, images, or symbols, be enhanced in vividness, complexity, or breadth of implication."[13] Tenor and vehicle are more closely drawn together and identified and metaphor is, thus, more dramatically concise (and, some would add, more powerful since the link words have been dropped): A is B.

In this play, all three of these figures can be found. We have already shown examples of comparison and simile, and we may discover metaphor in Hipólita's damning speech to Alvaro:

> Mal caballero, villano,
> que no es posible que sea
> de ilustre sangre quien es
> desagradecido, y deja
> de ser amigo por ser
> poderoso; ave funesta
> e ingrata, que al mismo dueño
> que le regala y alberga
> saca los ojos... (239b)

The move towards metaphorical expression in Calderón's theater is strongly underway.

In Saber, Calderón's growing control over imagery can be shown in an examination of the natural images. Much of the action of the play takes place in a "valle sombrío, al pie de un monte" (214a) or in "montes con peñascos cubiertos de matas" (235a). The natural setting is used to reflect the rising and falling fortunes of the two central characters. We may remember that Alvaro enters at the nadir of his fortunes, "despeñándose de un monte a los pies de las damas" (215a). At times the beauty of the natural setting is stressed and compared to the women who are called "ninfas del valle, diosas del bosque" (215b). Their beauty is further compared to "nieve, coral, fruta, flores." Natural images describe love and life, "es la vida un girasol" (221a) and Hipólita describes her feelings toward Alvaro in terms of a bee and a flower or a moth and a flame (227b - 228a). And nature, like love, has its negative side since love can turn to jealousy, "una flor ofrece al aspid / ponzoña" (228a).

Patterns of images are also beginning to be formed in this play. Besides the nature images, there is also a pattern of cosmic images. The King is the sun, women are stars, the moon is linked to fortune, and all the heavens enter through the vocabulary of the characters. This cosmic pattern seems to be used for two effects: first, to universalize the action, especially the action that deals with fortune, to make the portents of single acts more transcendant and encompassing in their effect, and second, to strengthen the play's overall tone.

The fact remains, however, that this comedia is still within the parameters of the early, youthful style because at times, for example, there is an inappropriateness between image and context. The most striking case of discordant imagery occurs near the beginning of the play. Alvaro enters fallen from the mountain, "muy herido y ensangrentado" (215a). He has just had a fight with the King's men over some food that he tried to take from the dogs since he was near starvation. Apparently, he has been severely wounded and the people who see him believe him near death. The mountain, the audience is told, will become his sepulcro and the oak his pirámide. He says that he cannot clearly see the women due to the "copioso raudal de sangre / de las heridas atroces" and, furthermore, he is "agonizando / en los brazos de la muerte" (215-216). As he falls at the women's feet, they employ a somewhat playful image, "y bañado / en el rojo humor que corre / de sus venas ya parecen / lengua de sangre las flores" (215a). That they can be so apparently unconcerned at the nobleman's condition is at first disconcerting. But as Alvaro himself looks at them through the blood covering his eyes, his, "Hermosísimas señoras / cuya voz, cuyas acciones / ninfas os dicen del valle, / diosas del bosque" (215b) is even more discordant. That a presumably dying man might utter such courtly phrases with what we at first suppose to be his dying gasps is more than one could expect for even the most polished gentleman. Immediately afterward, however, the audience learns that Alvaro has fully recovered and that what seemed to be mortal wounds were really trifles. Alvaro, the ladies, the King, and the audience believed that he was dying but when the audience sees him instantly recovered, it feels that it has been led astray by the poetic flourishes.

Besides the sense of disconnection between image and circumstance that is sometimes felt, there are also moments when the images used by one character evoke no response from those about him. In later plays, words and images pass from character to character and are changed and modified assuring their importance and their meaning, like a musical theme going through variations and inversions. Here, at times, images go unanswered. Alvaro uses a series of images in a love speech to Hipólita and Laura, "con alas de cera / he tocado la región del fuego... / es la vida un girasol / que tiene hermosura incierta" (221a), to which they prosaically reply, "¿Cómo os sentís?" In the later plays, one character will pick up and modify the images of another character as an indication not only that they are paying close attention to what those around them say, but also that they have developed differing attitudes or points of view and that the image has become the characteristic mode of speech used to achieve dramatic unity and economy.

We have noted significant changes in the five year period that separates <u>Judas Macabeo</u> from <u>Saber del mal y del bien</u>. Calderón has gained greater control over his art and we see the use of image patterns, tonal modulation, scenic design, and tighter structure in the focus of the play. Most of the images in the play are taken from nature and they are generally coordinated with the surrounding atmosphere, character, and theme. Though there are instances of disconnection, the imagery and techniques used here foretell the more functional imagery and the careful design that will become the hallmark of Calderón's mature style.

La dama duende

At the beginning of Act II of La dama duende (1629), Angela
has received an answer (the famous "Fermosa dueña, cualquiera que
vos seáis" letter) to the note she left for Don Manuel. She
says that she has never seen "tan cortés y galante / estilo"
(250a) and, after hearing the letter read, Beatriz also exclaims:

> ¡Buen estilo, por mi vida,
> y a propósito el lenguaje
> del encanto y la aventura! (250b)

Both women acknowledge that language and style serve particular
functions, reach particular goals. The chivalric, donquijotesque
language of the letter is perfect for an adventure with a
"magician."

In comparison, in the earlier plays many of the characters
spoke in essentially the same style and tone and used a common
vocabulary. It was quite difficult, for example, to separate the
Macabeo brothers on the basis of a particularized vocabulary. In
La dama duende, however, the audience does begin to recognize
characters by listening to how they express their feelings and
thoughts. Diction is a functional means of characterization.
But, before examining this aspect of the play in some detail, we
should look briefly at how style is also accommodated to the
general atmosphere and concerns of the work.

In the capa y espada plays, courtly language finds a home in
the gallant, bustling atmosphere of Madrid. The discrepancies
that were seen between action, ambience, and language in Saber do
not occur. Here, men should speak in gentlemanly tones, ladies
should be coquettish and a little adventurous, fathers and
brothers protective and on guard. But the atmosphere is also
exaggerated and since the lovers, especially the women, are young
and impetuous, the guardians are nearly fanatical. The tone and
structure is overtly comic. Danger lurks in dark encounters, but

the threat can be laughed away through love ending in marriage in the light of day. But it is this very recreation of court atmosphere that, on occasion, binds these plays in time and space to the contemporary Madrid scene and which, in turn, presents difficulties to the average reader. Later works transcend the momentary allusion and emphasize the human interest in settings that do not give rise to fleeting, localized comentary. It is not so much that the allusions trivialize interest in the play (allusions, for example in this play, to San Sebastian and other specific locales), but rather they may be small stumbling blocks in the reader's otherwise smooth though complex path.

As in most capa y espada plays, the possible loss of honor is ever present and the three main characters in this play, Angela, Manuel, and Luis, are constantly aware of this. Angela tells Manuel that the man following her (Luis) must not learn her identity because "Honor y vida me importa" (239a). Luis fears that the glass cupboard that separates Angela's room from Manuel's is too fragile to guard the family honor because "al primer golpe se quiebran / los vidrios" (242a). Isabel wonders about the man (Manuel) to whom Angela has entrusted her well-being, "a quien tu honor encargaste" (242b). Angela, in a letter, advises Manuel to proceed carefully for is she is discovered, "perderé yo el honor y la vida" (249a). And Manuel too realizes the danger to both "vida y honor" (265a) when he must hide in Angela's room.

Given the risks and surprises of La dama duende, characters find themselves in a constant state of wonder as things and events whirl about them. Their surprise is clearly shown in the use of recurrent exclamations such as ¡Vive el cielo!, ¡Vive Dios!, ¡Cielos!, ¡Válgame el cielo!, ¡Válgame Dios!, ¡Jesús!, and ¡Ay!." "¡Oh cielos!," exclaims Don Luis as he overhears Angela and Beatriz plotting to bring a man into the house (257b). Manuel, surprised at finding Cosme where he was never expected to be, cries, "¡Jesús mil veces!" (266a) in astonishment and, when

38

he sees the mysterious woman in his room, "¡Válgame el cielo!" (260a).

Despite the constant amazement of the characters, or perhaps because of it, they are always attempting to seek rational explanations for what is happening, all of them, that is, except for the superstitious Cosme for whom a rational explanation of the events is not necessary. The search for answers is, in part, what brings about much of the comedy in the play precisely because a reasonable solution for the mystery cannot be found through the logical means of hypothesis and deduction. This is true because the whole play turns on solving a riddle for which one must know the answer to find the answer.

Beatriz cannot imagine why a clever woman like Angela would be attracted to a man so obtuse that he cannot easily discover the moveable <u>alacena</u> which separates the rooms. But Angela reminds her that the solution is not nearly so easy as it appears to be:

> ¿Ahora sabes
> lo del huevo de Juanelo,
> que los ingenios más grandes
> trabajaron en hacer
> que en un bufete de jaspe
> se tuviese en pie, y Juanelo,
> con sólo llegar y darle
> un golpecillo, le tuvo?
> Las grandes dificultades,
> hasta saberse lo son;
> que sabido, todo es fácil. (252a)

Even before, in Act I, Isabel emphasized the riddle aspect of the play when she showed Angela how to enter and leave Manuel's room, adding "que solo la sepa abrir / el que lo llega a saber." (244b)

An atmosphere of seeking and questioning, of frustration and surprise is produced by the moveable alacena and by the attempts to discover the identity of the mysterious woman. This ambience is underscored by the iteration of the verb saber which, in one form or another, occurs 71 times in the play. Luis wants to know, "saber qué dama era aquella" (241a); and Manuel also exclaims "¡Vive Dios que he de saber quién es!" (261b). But Angela, until the very end of the play, is one step ahead of all the men. "Wait," she tells Manuel, and "mañana lo sabrás todo" (261a). Manuel never does completely decipher the riddle by himself and he must indeed wait until the final scene before everything is completely clarified, before the person who created the riddle comes in and gives him the complete answer.

Atmosphere, structure, and theme are supported by a common language used by all the characters but this does not mean that they always sound alike, for indeed they do not. The three principal characters have their own patterns of speech; patterns that, except for Manuel, are not particularly based on images, but rather on a standard diction. The characters, furthermore, are able to modulate and modify their speech patterns depending on the situation in which they find themselves and on the other characters to whom they are talking.

Luis is the most uncomplicated of the three and his basic vocabulary can be divided into three categories of words: those dealing with honor, those treating love, and those that show a negative attitude towards himself.

When it comes to the honor question, Luis is the most impetuous and the most anxious character in the play. He is ready to fight at a moment's notice (see Act I, 240a; Act III, 269b-270a and 272-b). He fears the fragile alacena and what it represents for his honor, "no ha puesto por defensa / de su honor más que unos vidrios, / que al primer golpe se quiebran" (242a). He returns home, upset, stating, "Harto tengo, tengo honor"

(243a). When he discovers Manuel hidden, Luis accuses him of mistreating the honor of the people who have trusted him (269a).

As it turns out, Luis' accusations are as rash as his actions. He is constantly running headlong into situations without pausing to consider whether what he has seen or heard is correct, a character trait that will appear in modifed versions in many of Calderón's later plays -- one recalls Don Gutierre in El médico de su honra and Segismundo in La vida es sueño for examples. When chasing after the mujer tapada in the first scenes of the play, Luis threatens Cosme, "os romperé la cabeza" (239b), pushes him (239b); is arrogant to Manuel; (240a) and ends up in a fight (240a). In the last act, he decides to find out who Angela and Beatriz are attempting to hide. Even he knows that his actions are rash, "Luz tomaré, aunque imprudente, / pues todo se halla con luz, / y el honor con luz se pierde" (268b). Luis trusts too much in his senses and this overconfidence, an attitude also to be observed in El Médico, is a cause for his downfall. "¿Quieres que mientan mis ojos?", he accusingly asks Don Manuel to which the more prudent gentleman responds with the playwright, "Sí, / que ellos engaño padecen / más que otro sentido" (269a).

Besides his rashness, Luis's other characteristic is a rather low opinion of himself. In a confessional speech to Rodrigo, he first says, "No hay acción que me suceda / bien" and then adds, "¡De mal anda mi fortuna!" (241b). His speeches are filled with negatives and with words of pain and suffering: atormentar, necio, agravio, desprecia, pesar, hiere, dolor, disgusto, descuidos, penas, desdén and he poetically asks Beatriz, "¿Soy la noche por ventura?" (252b). Luis even believes that his own family is plotting against him, "que cada día / mis hermanos a porfía / se conjuran contra mí" (253a).

Luis desperately wants to be loved by Beatriz but even here he has no luck as the lady loves only Don Juan, Luis's older brother. When Luis speaks of love, love is painful. His is "loco amor" (252b); love burns his heart, "abrasado de amor" (258a); love and jealousy are intimately connected in his speech, "amante y celoso yo" (254a); and if he cannot have love he will prevent others from having it (258a).

Through his actions and more particularly through his language Luis is presented as a hyperbolic, brash young man with a sometimes dangerous concept of honor for which he is more than willing to risk both his life and his family's name.

Manuel, against whom Luis twice draws his sword, is also concerned with his honor, but by comparing the two men we immediately see the differences. Where Luis is quick to resort to arms, Manuel would rather reason out the problem though he would never back away from a fight as is clearly shown in the play. Manuel shows a greater sense of respect for women, even for unknown women (239b), than does Luis and feels that he could never fail one who asked for his help, "no tengo de hacer / mal alguno a una mujer / que así de mí se fió" (249b).

On the other hand, there is something about Manuel that, perhaps because of his calm rationality, rings with a strong sense of practicality. When he must choose between staying in Madrid to find out more about the mysterious woman or going to Escorial to follow up his petition to the King, he says:

> pero uno importa al honor
> de mi casa y de mi aumento,
> y otro solamente a un gusto,
> y así entre los extremos,
> donde el honor es lo más,
> todo lo demás es menos. (287a)

The contrast between "aumento" and "gusto" could not be more striking as he reduces the love adventure to a brief and relatively unimportant diversion. But, for the play, it is precisely the adventure that is the most important element and events force Manuel to return to the house despite his desires to do otherwise. Whether he admits it or not, his contact with Angela has altered his life. He has been thrust into a world of chaos and confusion[14] from the first moments that he arrived in Madrid and the cause of the disorder is Angela.

Manuel employs a series of images of darkness to express his doubt and perplexity and these images are well adapted to the physical atmosphere in which many of his encounters with Angela take place -- in the darkened room at night. For example, he courageously agrees to meet an entourage sent by the mysterious woman at night and in a cemetary. In the brief monologue recounting the meeting, Manuel's speech is filled with words and images that reflect his innermost fears:

> Y al fin a un portal de horror
> lleno, de sombra y temor
> solo, y a oscuras salí.
> Aquí llegó una mujer
> (al óir y al parecer),
> y a oscuras y por el tiento,
> de aposento en aposento,
> sin óir, hablar ni ver,
> me guió. (263a, italics mine)

The link between darkness, fear, terror, and what appears to be a woman serving as guide is a partial summation of Manuel's entire adventure. This basically practical man bravely entrusts himself to an unknown woman for whom he risks his fortunes and his honor.

If images of darkness are one aspect of Manuel's speech, images of light are the other and, in fact, it is Manuel more than any other character who uses these images. All of the images of light are connected with his feelings about Angela. She is aurora, alba, arrebol, día, and sol who rescues him from "la noche oscura y fría" (263b). Her presence can abrasar,

alumbrar, amanecer, brillar, iluminar, and resplandecer. The key
speeches wherein the contrast between darkness and light, fear
and love can be observed occur at the beginning of Act III.
Manuel has been brought to the house, to the portal de horror
commented on above.   While waiting in a darkened room, he sees
light coming through the keyhole; his images change immediately
from dark, fearful ones to ones of surprise and beauty. First
Manuel alternates between descriptions of the women and the
house:

> ¡Qué casa tan alhajada!
> ¡Qué mujeres tan lucidas!
> ¡Qué sala tan adornada!
> ¡Qué damas tan bien prendidas!
> ¡Qué beldad tan extremada!   (263a)

and as Angela enters, he returns to a series of contrasts that
emphasize his change in feeling from fear to joy:

> La sombra ni el tornasol
> de la noche, no os había
> de estorbar: que sois el día... (263b)

> Huye la noche, señora
> y pasa a la dulce salva
> la risa bella del alba
> que ilumina... (263b)

> El alba, para brillar,
> quiso a la noche seguir;
> la aurora, para lucir,

al <u>alba</u> quiso imitar;
el <u>sol</u>, deidad singular,
a la <u>aurora</u> desafía,
vos al <u>sol</u>... (263b-64a)

Her beauty, his joy and release from fear are now joined in this
outpouring of light images that make the surrounding darkness
vanish. Metaphorically, Manuel always seeks the light as he
constantly searches for an explanation, a rational explanation,
for the mysteries that surround him in a cloak of confusion and
darkness. His language shows him to be noble and practical, at
times confused and fearful, but always willing to move carefully
ahead in search of the answer to the riddle.

To solve the riddle, however, Manuel must finally depend on
Angela because she controls almost everything in the play.[15] The
levels of her language are the most complex of all the characters
because she can modify her style at will and, depending on the
person to whom she is speaking, she can express fear, trust,
jealousy, curiosity, irony, mischief, and humility. In three
moments key to the understanding of her character she is humble,
intimate, and anguished.

In Act I, the first time we see her alone with Isabel, her
confidant, Angela's diction betrays a nearly hopeless sadness.
As she changes from the clothes she wore in the plaza to those
she must wear at home, she says:

Vuélveme a dar, Isabel,
esas tocas (¡pena esquiva!)
vuelve a amortajarme viva,
ya que mi suerte cruel
lo quiere así... (242a)

The vision she presents of a living death is then further accentuated when she expands her imagery from her clothing to her room, "Que yo entre dos paredes muera" and from the house to nature itself, "donde apenas el sol sabe / quién soy... donde inconstante la luna, / ... aprende influjos de mí..." (242). Angela must live "encerrada / sin libertad... porque enviudé de un marido, / con dos hermanos casada" (242b). The sadness and desperation that she feels caused by events beyond her control create the sense of living death from which she is attempting to escape.

In Act III, after Manuel's image-filled speech describing her as light, sun, dawn, Angela rejects each of his flowery compliments one by one and, in her rejection, defines her true nature:

> Y así os ruego que digáis
> señor Don Manuel, de m´
> que una mujer soy y fui... (264a)

but after this fleeting moment of soul-baring, she reverts to enigmatic language to confuse Manuel once again and to keep the game on track, "que no soy lo que parezco / ni parezco lo que soy" (264a). For it is only in the last scenes where Angela can finally tell Manuel precisely who she is (partly because events have closed in around her and she has lost control of the game), confess her true feeling, solve the riddle, and ask his love and help one last time:

> Por haberte querido
> fingida sombra de mi casa he sido;
> por haberte estimado
> sepulcro vivo fui de mi cuidado;
> porque no te quisiera,
> quien el respeto a tu valor perdiera:

```
porque no te estimara
quien su pasión dijera cara a cara.
Mi intento fue el quererte,
mi fin amarte, mi temor perderte,
mi miedo aseguarte,
mi vida obedecerte...
mi llanto, en efecto, persuadirte
que mi daño repares,
que me valgas, me ayudes y me ampares. (271b)
```

Herein she unites the images of darkness and mystery with words of love, respect, fear, and true intention. She submits to him as she confesses her love and asks his aid in her moment of need. Manuel, given his character, can do nothing other than accept even if his acceptance is more out of duty than out of love: "Y para cumplir mejor / con la obligación jurada, / a tu hermana doy la mano" (272b, emphasis mine).

Angela's intimate confessions contrast vividly with the various ways that the other characters have described her. In comparing what she says with what the others say about her, we find that none of them truly understood her completely. Cosme, the most incorrect of all, believes that she is a duende (a word, taken with duendecillo, that he uses 27 times, 9 times more than that of any other character), demonio, or diablo (a word only he uses). Luis calls her hermana, as does Juan, but for the younger man, she is also the mujer tapada and a co-conspirator with Beatriz (257b-258a). Juan feels that his sister must be guarded because she, along with all women, is fickle and lighthearted. When he catches her dressed in finery, Angela easily deceives him saying that she is dressed thus to relieve her sadness to which Juan chauvinistically responds:

```
No lo dudo;
que tristezas de mujeres
bien con galas se remedian,
```

bien con joyas convalecen... (265a)

At several points in the play, Manuel thinks that he knows who she is, but each time he is wrong. At first, she must be Luis' wife (239b); then his dama (249a); then he does not know what, "aquella, / no es su dama; porque él / despreciado no viviera, si en su casa la tuviera" (254a). Near the end of Act II, Manuel nearly falls into Cosme's belief in superstition, "Ya es / esto sobrenatural" (260a) he exclaims as Angela uncovers a lamp in his room just as he mentions his need for light, but almost immediately he sees how beautiful she is and decides that she is an "ángel hermoso" (260b). When Angela subsequently "disappears" his doubts return, but now, at least, he is sure that she is human and female because she showed fear when he drew his sword. In the visit to her house at night, Manuel believes her a rich noblewoman (264b). His confusion is never clarified until Angela herself tells him who she is.

As we can now observe, the principal image patterns of the play are two and they both center on Angela: light-darkness and angel-devil. The language of the male characters shows their constant search for a solution to the mysteries that surround them as it also betrays their beliefs and their natures. The search itself revolves around the polar contrast of saber / confusión as these linguistic elements accentuate the appearance vs. reality theme so well-developed in the work. Deceit, role play, and riddles all contribute their share to the creation of the capa y espada atmosphere of which La dama duende is a prime example.

To emphasize that characters in this play, through their own peculiarities of vocabulary choice, characterize themselves, there are two final items that we shall examine: first, the personal pronouns yo and me (me acting as a direct or indirect object but not as a reflexive pronoun) and second, Angela's use of ser. Depending on the usage of the pronouns, characters may be classed as doers (active characters who do things to others) and or receivers (those to whom things are done).

Of the three principal characters, Luis, Angela, and Manuel, Luis uses yo in an active sense more than the others. When chasing the unknown woman he says, "Yo tengo que conocerla" (239b) followed by several first person verbs of action, voy, romperé , respondo. He tells Angela about his adventure saying, "Yo las seguí" (243b) and "Iba de prisa, entré en la plaza, A un coro me fui, adonde vi, llegué" This active quality in Luis' descriptions of his own action and in his speech in general underlines his rash, headlong leaps from situation to situation, from error to error.

Manuel, for contrast, is more the receiver of the actions of others than a doer. This has already been suggested when we said that he was in a constant state of surprise and bewilderment. He uses me 49 times in the play and he is the receiver of an action in all but eight cases. He was honored by the Duque de Feria (me honró", 238b); he asks Cosme how he can doubt that Manuel would help the young lady, "¿eso me preguntas?" (239b); he can be found whenever Luis wishes, "me hallaréis donde quisieseis" (240b); he is pained by his reception in Madrid, "Qué tristeza / me ha dado que me reciba / con sangre Madrid" (241a); he praises Luis, "en todo me vencéis" (245b) and hopes that Luis' sword will show him how to act, "me enseñe a ser valiente" (245b); the mysterious appearance of Angela's note "me suspende" (249a); when Cosme says that the doors and windows are locked so that no one could have entered thus into the room, "Con mayor duda me dejas / y mil sospechas me dan" (249b); he says that an unknown woman "me guió" (263a); and, for the offer of help from Luis, he thanks him "por la merced que me hacéis" (263a).

Angela's use of yo and me, in terms of frequency of occurrence, points out that she is at the same time a doer and a receiver as befits her role in the play. She can actively exploit her role as the mysterious woman and, in so doing, take

the lead as actor. She decides to enter Manuel's rocm, "quiero /
a esotro cuarto pasar" (244b); she wrote the note to Manuel, "Yo
te escribí aquesta tarde" (261); she leaves the house at night,
"mi casa dejo..." (270b) "a caminar empiezo" (271a); she escapes
danger, "me escapé del modo / que te dije" (257a); and she will
cause Manuel more and more confusion "que me vea del modo que te
digo, / ni dudo de que pierda el juicio" (257a). But she is also
controlled by her brothers, by her role in the society, and in
part by the very game that she has chosen to play. Isabel, for
example, inadvertently closes her in Manuel's room, "me ha
cerrado Isabel" (262a); she fears that Manuel will reject her if
he discovers who and what she is "quiza me aborreceréis"
(264b).

The other interesting element that we can observe about
Angela's yo is in connection with the verb ser. She is a protean
character defining and redefining herself, all of which may be
counterposed to Manuel's frantic attempts to discover her true
identity. At first Angela wants to hide her identity from Luis,
"me importa / que aquel hidalgo no sepa / quien soy" (239b).
After adopting the role of dama duende, she is amused that Manuel
believes her to be Luis's lover (252a). In keeping with the
riddle, she presents a series of enigmatic identities, "un enigma
a ser me ofrezco / que ni soy lo que parezco / ni parezco lo que
soy" (264a). Without telling Manuel what she is, Angela does
tell him what she is not, "no soy / alba, aurora o sol" (264a),
and then she gives him the simplest and most touching answer,
"que una mujer soy" (264a). In the last scenes, she does
eventually tell him who she is and why she has done what she did,
"Don Juan, mi hermano... / que ya resisto, ya defiendo en vano /
decir quien soy" (271a). She is, then, both the exploited and
the exploiter who enters the game for diversion and later finds
love. Angela moves from mystery to revelation through a series
of disguises and identities which she forges but also which at
times are forged for her.

In <u>La</u> <u>dama</u> <u>duende</u>, Calderón, through the judicious use of certain personalized vocabulary items, has been able to delineate individual characters and their personalities. This play marks a transition between the first period in his development and the second in which he will write his most widely known works. Here, diction creates character while in <u>Casa</u> <u>con</u> <u>dos</u> <u>puertas</u>, different results for differing purposes are achieved through the exploitation of other linguistic possibilities.[16]

Casa con dos puertas mala es de guardar

In his introduction to La Dama duende's twin play, Casa con
dos puertas mala es de guardar (1629), Angel Valbuena Briones
says that one of the differences between the two plays is that
the former is an original and that the latter is really a copy
perhaps written in haste to take advantage of the outstanding
popularity of La dama duende (273a). Nevertheless, Casa con dos
puertas is, as Valbuena suggests, a unified, well-constructed
play. In structural terms, we may note that there are two plots,
two groups of characters linked by friendship, two houses with
two doors each, two "father figures," and three triangles based
on love -- Lisardo, "mujer tapada," Félix; Félix, "bulto,"
Laura; Laura, Nice, Félix. There are two "mujeres tapadas" both
of whom are Marcela. Marcela is the controlling presence, the
comic pointer who is never deceived by the actions of the others.
We have mirror scenes and mirror scenes within mirror scenes all
of which tend to give a sense of order to the seemingly confusing
action. As in La dama duende, in Casa con dos puertas we have
all of the characteristic, complicated elements of a capa y
espada play.

Typically, deceit moves the two plots as Marcela tricks
Lisardo, Félix, and Laura to keep the game alive and to try to
avoid early discovery in her efforts to marry Lisardo. But in a
much more impertinent fashion than in the earlier play, the
female protagonist jeopardizes her friends', her relatives', and
her own honor to achieve her personal ends. In Act II, for
example, she imprudently invites Lisardo to visit her in Laura's
house thereby fooling him about where she (Marcela) lives.
Moreover, she risks Laura's honor and her friend is rightfully
angered, "Detente, espera; / que has usado neciamente, / Marcela,
de la licencia / de la amistad" (288a). In general, the
characters in this work are more reckless, more mean to each
other than those in La dama duende. Here, they are willing to
deceive, to lie, to cheat, to risk each other's honor for the
achievement of personal goals.[17]

Though the atmosphere of imprudence is more strong in this work than in the earlier one, the similarities, as suggested above, are quite striking. As in the techniques and in the staging, there are also many echoes of La dama duende in the image patterns. We can note the standard love imagery whereby women are compared to the stars and to the sun (285b); relations between lovers are described as those of sol to girasol, imán to piedra, and mariposa to llama (276a/b, 279a).

There is a strongly rhetorical flavor to several of the speeches which seem to be, at times, more exercises in logic than expressions of true feelings (see, for example, p. 285a, "O tienes celos o no..."). This rhetorical quality recalls passages from earlier plays. In this work, Calderón has often separated speeches from the natural flow of conversation as he did in Judas Macabeo by using such disjunctive phrases as "escucha" (288a), "discurramos" (278a), "escuchadme" (278b), "oye atenta" (286b), and "oye" (293b).

We also find many examples of the "epic simile" as in Judas Macabeo, and in Saber del mal y del bien and conjunctive phrases that link the image overtly to the context, "pues así," " y así," " yo así," " como," " bien como" (276b, 279a, 279b, 285b). At the end of Act I, for example, Félix is trying to dissuade Laura from her belief that he still loves Nise. To do so, he uses an image that will appear later in El médico de su honra,

> Pues explíqueme mejor
> otro ejemplo: nace ciego
> un hombre, y discurre luego
> cómo será el resplandor
> del sol, planeta mayor,
> que rumbos de zafir gira;
> y cuando por fe le admira,
> cobra en una noche bella

```
          la vista; y es una estrella
          la primer cosa que mira.
          Admirando el tornasol
          de la estrella, dice: "Sí.
          éste es el sol; que yo así
          tengo imaginado al sol";
          pero cuando su arrebol
          tanta admiración le ofrece,
          sale el sol, y le oscurece...
          Yo así, que ciego vivía
          de amor, cuando no te amaba... (285b)
```

In his image, he creates a story in which a character does a series of actions, reaches a series of conclusions and then he, the speaker, applies that story and that character's situation to his own.

Certain aspects of the central image patterns do distinguish Casa con dos puertas from La dama duende. The major images in both plays are focused on love and they arise from the natural, physical surroundings in which the characters move. In La dama duende, the images of clothing, of ángel/demonio, of light/dark led to a discovery of Angela's identity as did the confusion/knowledge motif. In Casa con dos puertas, the images point to a more profound discussion than that of identity; they lead to a consideration of the inherent duality of reality, a discussion that will arise many times in Calderón's career. For the characters in this work, love is a major feature of reality, and love is contradictory in its essence. Through the eyes of these characters, we see love as both pain and pleasure and the equality of these and other contraries is noted throughout:

```
          porque de amor el veneno
          cure triaca de amor (302b)
Lau:                    Félix mío,
```

```
              mi bien, mi señor, mi dueño.
       Fel:   Mi mal, mi muerte, mi ofensa... (292b)

              que no pueden ser iguales
              en el mundo dos efectos,
              si de una causa no nacen (280a)
```

Nature and the garden imagery that arises in scenes where
the characters meet in the natural surroundings is also dual.
The garden imagery is part of an archetypal pattern reflecting a
Garden of Eden. Eden was both a paradise for man and the hiding
place for the serpent, "pues áspid, que no deidad, es / quien da
muerte entre las flores" (277a). The garden, like love, encloses
the dual realities of happiness and sadness, of life and death.

The garden is compared to the sea which is called an
"inconstante selva" (287a). And the sea also shows two realities
to man:

```
              el mar desde afuera,
              convidando con la paz
              a cuantos a verle llegan,
              cuando jugando las ondas
              unas con otras se encuentran,
              pues el que más confiado
              pisó su inconstante selva,
              ése lloró más perdido
              la saña de sus ofensas (287b)
```

Marcela then compares the two aspects of the sea, one of peace
and of invitation, the other of disaster and death, to love, "Yo
así apacible juzgué / el mar del amor; pero apenas / reconocí
sus halagos, / cuando sentí sus violencias" (287b).

Yet despite this insight into the dual nature of reality,
the imagery that conveys it is not as well developed in this play

as it was in La dama duende. In the earlier play, the images were in constant use by all of the principal characters. Hardly a speech passed without reference to the central image patterns or to the motifs to which they were bound. In Casa con dos puertas, we do not find the consistency of usage that we do in La dama duende. For instance, Act III begins with references to nature in the conversation between Marcela and Laura, but in the following conversation between Lisardo and Calabazas, and from there to the end of the act, there are no images from the patterns established beforehand. Action predominates in the last scenes and imagery is dropped. This is not to say, however, that images do not pass from hand to hand in other parts of the play for they certainly do at times. Note, for example, how Laura, at the end of Act I, picks up the celestial imagery used by Félix and turns it to her own purposes or how Marcela does the same thing with Lisardo's imagery at the beginning of the same act. What we find, nonetheless, is little consistency in this phenomenon.

It seems in this play that Calderón develops his images in the longer passages where the pace is slower and, therefore, allows for more introspection and for more development on the part of the speaker. This suggests, then, that images here flourish only in certain situations and not in others and that perhaps imagery and action are not working as closely together as they could. One possible reason is, as Valbuena Briones suggested, that the play was written in haste and that even though the images point to more profound concerns, they are not as well integrated into the very fabric of the play as possible or even as was the case in La dama duende.

On the other hand, one of the most striking notes about the imagery in the present play is the rise of associative images in those speeches wherein imagery predominates. We can contrast this technique with the "cadenas de imágenes" that Valbuena Prat speaks of in his studies of Calderón s works. The difference is

that an image chain is a list of parallel images like the sol-
girasol, norte-imán pairs that we find at the beginning of the
play; while associative imagery would be that found in a passage
where one word suggests to the poet another word or image that is
not just a parallel example in another voice, but rather an
outgrowth of the first. Images are being formed, as it were, in
the very act of composition. If we examine the sea-love imagery
used by Félix in Act I, we can clearly see this technique at
work. Here, the key is the use of "viento en popa":

> Desta suerte, pues, teniendo
> la Fortuna de mi parte,
> viento en popa del amor
> corrí los inciertos mares
> hasta que el viento mudado
> levantaron huracanes
> de una tormenta de celos,
> montes de dificultades.
> Tormenta de celos dije:
> ved, si alguna vez amasteis,
> ¿qué esperanza hay del piloto?
> ¿Qué seguro de la nave? (280a)

Here, "viento en popa", meaning "going very well" gives rise to
the notion of the sea and then to the fate of a ship tossed about
by the uncertain winds of a storm. Both the ship and the captain
are in danger of losing all. Calderón has seen the
relationship, the similarity based on danger between the lover,
the pilot of the ship, and the craft he controls and from that
perspective, he creates the images. Images appear naturally, not
only out of comparisons to physical surroundings but also to
states of mind. Parallel to the above passage is another love
speech on 285b where the key word "estudiar" leads to the use of

"ciencias," "ensayo," "estudio," "universidad," "libros" and another passage based on "luz" on the same page.

As images arise out of one word or one phrase, so also in this play do images become transformed in the process of using them:

> flecha disparada al aire,
> y no por venganza flecha
> bañada en venenos tales,
> que salió del arco pluma,
> corrió por el viento ave,
> luego rayo al corazón,
> donde se alimienta áspid [279a]

The image of love begins as an arrow and ends as an asp. The relation between the two is that of wounding deeply, of stinging, and of possible death. Each successive image is related to its immediate predecessor. In the air, the arrow, because of the feathers on the end and because it flies through the air, becomes a bird winging its way to its goal. Because of the speed of the arrow/bird, it is transformed into a "rayo", more unexpected, more swift, more powerful. It strikes the heart where it takes up residence as an asp. The asp creates the suggestion of poison which, in turn, takes us back to the third line, "venenos." The image, unlike the chains of images and unlike the image lists in Judas Macabeo, achieves a climax with the last element and it is unified, clarified, and transformed in the process.

These observations on Casa con dos puertas, show that on the one hand, there are still standardized images in use throughout the play but that on the other, the imagery is not only more organic to the physical situation but also to the mental state of the characters. Some images arise from association with others and some undergo certain modifications in the process of building to a climax. As in La dama duende,

Calderón is carefully linking images and using patterns to signal his thematic concerns. The central images affirm the conflicting duality of nature as they stress reality conceived of as an interplay of opposites. This trend toward a balancing of effects, toward reality portrayed as dual, will be more strongly manifest in some of his later works but even at this transition point, Calderón's inclination in that direction is clear.

Introduction to Part II

In the 1630-1650 period, Calderón's imagery becomes more organic, more concise, more balanced, and more complex. It forms a current that runs throughout an entire play and, is ever present instead of bubbling up only in moments of high emotion or of crisis. At the same time, the bond between imagery and atmosphere, character, theme, and structure becomes unbreakable.

In the middle period, patterns are the predominant way of presenting images. Robert B. Heilman, speaking of Shakespeare's imagery, defines a pattern as "a combination or system of poetic and dramatic elements which can be shown to work together in encompassing a body of meaning that has a place in the over-all structure of the play."[18] The focus, while perhaps starting with the single or repeated image, inevitably shifts to a wider design that includes character, theme, and structure. The image is not limited to a single scene or to a fleeting speech, but rather is prepared for and emphasized by other parallel images that cohere around a central subject: around medicine, night, sight, dreams or whatever. These patterns are realized both verbally and poetically in the speeches and visually and physically in the actions. Thus, for example, dark images may lead to the extinguishing of a candle. The dramatic action and the poetic pattern, as says in another context, "are reciprocally illuminating and animating; they are interdependent in the manner of the parts of an organism; together they form rich and stimulating patterns of meaning" (p. 25).

While remembering the parallel listing of images in Judas Macabeo, let us look at the organic growth of image from image that characterizes the plays of the middle period. As in parts of Casa con dos puertas, in these middle plays too, one word sets off a chain reaction of images that extend throughout the play beyond the situation at hand. Notice Mencía's speech in El médico de su honra:

> ¡Oh quién pudiera dar voces,
> y romper con el silencio
> cárceles de nieve, donde
> está aprisionado el fuego,
> que ya, resuelto en cenizas,
> es ruina que está diciendo:
> ¡Aquí fue amor! (318b)

From her inner anguish, Mencía cries out privately what she
cannot declare publicly (she cries out, that is, until she
remembers "yo soy quien soy"). From this desire to unburden her
soul arises the idea of breaking the silence (the taboos, the
prison of time, the prison of social responsibility) that
surrounds her. This silence encloses her long dormant emotions
like icy prisons. The movement from the desire to shout out to
the requirement for silence and from past to present demonstrates
clearly the internal battle beginning to rage in her breast.

Just beneath the cold surface that she must maintain lies
imprisoned, aprisionado, the fire that can melt these snowy bars.
Aprisionado echoes cárceles and grows from the idea of breaking
out in romper, and that in turn from dar voces. She hastens to
add, however, that the fire is now ashes, and then ruins, of that
past love. The intimate connection of fire, ashes, and ruins is
explicit. Yet these ruins, like ruins of past civilizations,
have a power to speak across the years to tell, "¡Aquí fue
amor!" The interrelated imagery, at times parallel -- dar voces-
romper con el silencio --, at times in opposition -- voces-
silencio, nieve-fuego --, follows an exact order. There is a
crescendo of emotion, of concealed feelings that burst forth
uncontrollably toward the final declaration of love. We cannot
vary the order without irreparably harming the entire passage.

Conciseness too will become a hallmark of the imagery in the
middle plays. We can point to few rambling passages or, indeed,
to hardly any sections of these works that do not contribute to

advancing some major concern of the drama. This compactness demonstrates the growing move toward more functional imagery already forseen in La dama duende and Casa con dos puertas. And, since drama is a time-limited genre, conciseness is a major virtue.

By comparing two selections, the first from Casa con dos puertas and the second from El médico de su honra, we can observe the succinctness of the later passage:

Casa con dos puertas

Pues explíqueme mejor
otro ejemplo: nace ciego
un hombre, y discurre luego
cómo será el resplandor
del sol, planeta mayor
que rumbos de zafir gira;
y cuando por fe le admira,
cobra en una noche bella
la vista, y es una estrella
la primer cosa que mira.
Admirando el tornasol
de la estrella, dice, "Sí,
éste es el sol; que yo así
tengo imaginado al sol";
pero cuando su arrebol
tanta admiración le ofrece
sale el sol y le oscurece.
Pregunto yo; ¿ofenderá
una estrella que se va,
a todo un sol que amanece?
Yo así que ciego vivía
de amor, cuando imaginaba
cómo aquel amor sería:

adoraba lo que vía,
presumiendo que era así
el amor; mas, ¡ay de mi!,
que no vi al sol, vi una estrella,
y entretúveme con ella,
hasta que el sol mismo vi.

And from El médico:

Escúchame un argumento:
Una llama en noche oscura
arde hermosa, luce pura,
cuyos rayos, cuyo aliento
dulce ilumina del viento
la esfera; sale el farol
del cielo, y a su arrebol
toda la sombra se reduce
ni arde, ni alumbra, ni luce;
que es mar de rayos el sol.
Aplico ahora: yo amaba
una luz, cuyo esplendor
vivió planeta mayor,
que sus rayos sepultaba:
una llama me alumbraba;
pero era una llama aquella,
que eclipsas divina y bella
siendo de luces crisol;
porque hasta que sale el sol
parece hermosa una estrella.

First the similarities: the contexts are parallel in that both Félix of Casa and Gutierre of El médico attempt to show Laura and Mencía, respectively, that the women need not feel jealous about the man's past loves; there is a rhetorical frame

in which the images are set, "Pues explíqueme mejor / otro
ejemplo--Escúchame un argumento", and, "Yo así que ciego
vivía--Aplico ahora"; the image pattern is parallel in the use
of the stars, the sun, the light-dark contrast; and finally, of
course, both passages deal with the love theme. But though the
selections are similar, there are striking differences that point
to the growing mastery of the techniques of poetic drama.

The concision of the second passage as opposed to the more
discursive nature of the first is impressive. The earlier
quotation can be characterized by the use of rhetorical
questions, both overt and implied: "¿ofenderá / una estrella
que se va, / a todo un sol que amanece?; ¿cómo será el
resplandor / del sol; / cómo aquel amor sería." Rhetorical
questions do not call for a response nor for a reaction on the
part of the listener. In the first passage, furthermore, a
fictionalized character has been interposed between Félix and
his emotions, "nace ciego / un hombre" followed by an interior
dialogue as the created character speaks to himself, "dice: 'Sí,
/ éste es el sol...'" There are also poetic embellishments,
"que rumbos de zafir gira" and exclamations in the first that do
little to advance the message. In fact, the entire quotation
from Casa con dos puertas is set up like an extended simile, more
digressive in nature than a metaphor. The use of such words as
así, como, cómo, signal the passage as a simile.

In the later treatment, the speaker begins not with a
comparison but with a metaphor, "una llama en noche oscura / arde
hermosa." He then compares this flame to the sun and concludes
that the flame, though originally thought bright, pales to
insignificance when placed beside the sun. Without stating
directly that Laura, his past love, is the flame and Mencía, his
true love, is the sun, the reader and Mencía easily follow his
logical and more compact development. Then, without the
intervention of a fictitious third person ("un hombre" in the

first selection), Gutierre states sincerely his own feelings, "yo amaba."

We could continue to make our case by connecting the images in the later passage, sol, llama, luz, noche, eclipsas, to the central image pattern of the play and to show how they lead us slowly , but inexorably, to predict Mencía's death when, at the end of the play, she becomes a "sol eclipsado", but the point has been made. The second passage is tighter, more dramatically integrated into the fabric of the play, and it is more straightforward in its presentation though more suggestive at the same time.

In the middle plays too, man stands in an intimate relationship with nature. We need only think of Segismundo in the cave (La vida es sueño), of Gutierre and the night (El médico de su honra), of El Tetrarca and the monstrous environment that surrounds him (El mayor monstruo del mundo) or of Don Alvaro and the sea (El pintor de su deshonra) to remember just how much nature is with the characters in the major plays.

In El alcalde de Zalamea, for example, Pedro Crespo is in close contact with the peaceful aspects of the natural order. This relationship also extends to his daughter, Isabel. Even after she has been raped and abandoned by the Capitán, she portrays her anguish by calling on nature to aid her:

> Nunca amanezca a mis ojos
> la luz del hermoso día,
> porque a su sombra no tenga
> vergüenza yo de mí misma.
> ¡Oh tú, de tantas estrellas
> primavera fugitiva,
> no des lugar a la aurora,
> que tu azul campaña pisa,
> para que con risa y llanto
> borre tu apacible vista...

>Detente, oh mayor planeta,
>más tiempo en la espuma fría
>del mar... (560a)

Nature, the sun, the night, the stars become compassionate witnesses to Isabel's dishonor. She calls for a reversal of the natural order and for a cessation of natural law since she no longer can be a part of the beauty of nature and because, for her, order can never return to normal. She wants the night to hold back the sun so that she may live in exterior darkness that can match and harmonize with her interior darkness. She fears the light which will reveal her shame. But the imagery does not stop with this comparison. As a child of nature, Crespo's daughter, she sees her own attributes in terms of nature. She conceives of her past honor as "la clara luna limpia de mi honor" which today "tan torpe mancha le eclipsa." She has become, in her own concept, as black as the night to which she has appealed. This inner harmony is more than "atmosphere", it is an organic, living relationship between man and nature.

Yet Isabel is not just a single example in the work, for as Peter Dunn notes, "Crespo is a man who seeks and celebrates what is harmonious and orderly in Nature"[19] ; the Capitán turns "to the dark and labyrinthine side of Nature for complicity" (p. 20); while Rebolledo, La Chispa, and Don Mendo show "nature prostituted, Law turned to self-assertion." (p. 22)

The dramas of this period also contain striking, new metaphors of great beauty and power. Because of the conciseness achieved in these plays, at times, Calderón must compress a wealth of feelings and meanings into a few words. And, often, because of the speed with which the action must proceed, he does not have the time to spin out an image and so he turns to these stunning metaphors to suggest many possibilities of interpretation. In La devoción de la cruz, Julia, crying over her dead brother's wounds declares, "que al fin heridas y ojos /

son bocas que nunca mienten" (399b). As the blood flows from the wounds and the tears from her eyes, the blood and tears speak, silently but openly, of the sadness, anger, and frustration she feels because of his death. The openings of the eyes and the wounds are compared to a mouth as the tears and blood are the words that issue forth. In Gustos y disgustos no son más que imaginación , we find a fascinating analogy between the sun and a jealous lover that both expresses the atmosphere of the play and the feelings of the major male character. Don Vivante had been all night in the street below Violante's window and would still be there, we are told,

> y hasta ahora se estuviera,
> si el sol, celoso y amante,
> a cuchilladas de luces
> no le echara de la calle (II, 972a)

Characters in the plays of this period do not speak in isolation from either the atmosphere of the work or from the other characters around them. The fact that one character picks up and modifies an image used by another shows that they are paying close attention to what others around them are saying. This congruency underscores the dramatic cohesion we have already pointed out. In El pintor de su deshonra, for example, Don Alvaro reminds Serafina that whereas previously she was a "girasol" to his love and an "edificio" wherein his love existed, she is now "al agua y al viento / dura encina, escollo altivo" (882b). Serafina then takes his image stating:

> No lo niego; mas también,
> si me valgo dese indigno
> concepto que contra mí
> hallaron tus desvarios,
> de esa humilde fácil flor

> hacer el tiempo ha podido,
> con las raíces que ha echado
> dentro de mi pecho invicto,
> inmortal tronco, y también
> de ese amoroso edificio
> caduca ruina. (882b)

Adding her perspective and noting the ignoble quality of his speech, Mencía refers to the "concepto" used by Alvaro. Parting from the "flower" comparison, she says that time, a major theme in this work, has made the flower take such deep roots that it has become a trunk, an immortal trunk able to withstand the new pressure that he seeks to exert against her. And, she adds, the building has fallen to ruins again due to the passage of time. Thus she has taken Alvaro's image and modified it in such a way as to turn the attack against her to a defense of her new status and her virtue.

We will see too that the bond between image and theme becomes unbreakable. We need only think of the ties between the dream as action, the dream as image, and the dream as concept in La vida es sueño or of the medical imagery and its links to honor and death in El médico de su honra. The very titles of many of the plays in this period point to the bond between the metaphor and the theme, for example, El pintor de su deshonra, La desdicha de la voz, La devoción de la cruz.

In La devoción de la cruz, the image of the cross is omnipresent. It is used at times humorously as when Gil enters "con muchas cruces y una muy grande al pecho" stating:

> Que de la cruz dicen que es
> devoto Eusebio, y así
> he salido armado aquí
> de la cabeza a los pies (410a)

At other times the reference is more serious. Eusebio explains
how the cross, this time a cross in the road, saved his life:

> En tanto que me quedé
> haciendo oración en ella /en una cruz/
> se adelantó el compañero;
> y después, dándome prisa
> para alcanzarle, le hallé
> a poco espacio de tierra,
> agonizando en su sangre,
> muerto a las manos sangrientos
> de bandoleros... (394a)

The mark of the cross, as we are told, has been imprinted on his
chest since birth. His constancy to the symbol saves his soul
since through the intercession of the cross, he is permitted to
confess even after death:

> Después de haber muerto Eusebio,
> el Cielo despositó
> su espíritu en su cadáver,
> hasta que se confesó;
> que tanto con Dios alcanza
> de la Cruz la devoción (419b)

The process of development from image to leitmotif to symbol and
the close ties between image and theme is manifest in all the
plays from this period.

An examination of the imagery in the principal plays of
these years helps us appreciate the play as a dynamic, living
organism in which image, theme, structure, atmosphere, character,
all of the dramatic elements are harmonized. Each of the plays
has its own unmistakable sound. All of the details are balanced
and tuned and the imagery of these works looks ahead to the

future and then looks back to past and present events drawing each aspect of the work into a closer relationship with each other element. The imagery that appears in one character's speech is echoed, in another key, by other characters. The imagery that appears in Act I is changed, developed, made more meaningful in the second act and finally brought to execution in the final one. Imagery plays a key role in binding together all of the various elements that make up the great plays of the 1630-1650 period.

El mayor monstruo del mundo

Recurrent imagery is one of the most effective techniques that a dramatist has at his command to create tone and atmosphere. The focus here on recurrent words, is not to make lists of them, but rather to see how they work in the structure of meaning in El mayor monstruo del mundo. Recurrency of words, as has already been seen, is a fact and a skillful dramatist would not repeat a word or a series of words, beyond what was absolutely necessary due to plot or sense, if it were not, for his purposes, important. It matters little whether the iteration is conscious or unconscious for the mere fact that they are repeated endows the words with special values. The repetition of the verb ver, for example, makes the audience aware of the importance of sight in general terms and they must try to discover its role in the play.

There will probably be more than one of these patterns in any given play and besides investigating the role of the single metaphor or of the single word within the individual pattern, the audience must also try to understand the relationships among the various patterns in the whole play. This organic patterning is a much more subtle and powerful use of imagery than that achieved through the imagery which, in earlier plays, was confined to particular scenes.

In El mayor monstruo del mundo (1634), the way the characters see and describe their world tells as much about the space in which they exist as about the speakers themselves. In this play, characters employ three related image patterns that reveal their world and self concepts: images of nature, of prisons, and of disorder. These patterns show how they see the world as circumscribed space that grows more horrifying and claustrophobic as the action of the play develops.

In the nature pattern there are a large number of celestial references which serve two fundamental ends: they focus the audience's attention on the influence of the prophecy read in the stars and they underscore the pervasive sense of fatalism and despair that nearly all of the characters express. Mariene saw her fate written in the skies:

> que es todo el cielo
> depósito infeliz de mi desvelo,
> pues todo el cielo escribe
> mi desdicha, que en él grabada vive
> en papel de cristal con letras de oro... (454a)

> el mayor monstruo del mundo
> mi vida amenaza en ese
> firmamento encuadernado (459a)

Through imagery, Mariene herself becomes part of the very cosmic order that she so fears again. Following standard usage, El Tetrarca compares his beautiful wife to the sun, but as the play progresses, she becomes "un sol sin luz" (474a) and Octaviano, early on, establishes a relationship between the sun and death (465b). The menacing aspect of the cosmos and the link forged between Mariene, the sun, and death all serve to prefigure ther tragic end. As the play closes, Octaviano adds her epitaph in celestial imagery calling her a "cielo caduco" and saying that they have seen "¡eclipsado al sol mas puro!" (489b)[20].

The sun and light images can be contrasted with a series of darker ones that, to help prepare the rapidly approaching deaths, become predominant in the last scenes of the play. There is, then, a trajectory in the imagery from the first scenes where light images, the countryside, and peaceful nature are in evidence:

> La divina Mariene,
> el sol de Jerusalén,
> por divertir tus tristezas,

```
vio el campo al amanecer.
Las aves, fuentes y flores
le dan dulce parabién,
repitiendo por servirla,
al aire, una y otra vez:
Sea triunfo de sus manos
lo que es pompa de sus pies.
Fuentes, sus espejos sed
corred, corred, corred.
Aves su luz saludad
volad, volad.
Flores, pasó prevenid,
vivid, vivid. (458a/b)
```

to the last scenes which take place more and more in the darknesses of prisons, in the semiobscurity of enclosed rooms, and in the blackness of night:

```
¿Tú en una oscura prisión,
funesto, y mísero albergue...? (II, 479a)
```

```
        ...para salir
hoy de duelo tan injusto
he de apagar la luz.
(Anda a cuchilladas y mata la luz) (III,489a)
```

In the final scene when Octaviano goes to free Mariene, he enters when "el ave nocturno / extiende las alas negras / haciendo sombras" (486b-87a). The anthropomorphic reference to night can be tied to the frightening aspects of nature which we will treat in a later section. The atmosphere created by the nocturnal bird that covers the earth with its dark wings is at the same time an intensification of the blackness of night, with emphasis falling on nocturno, negras, and sombras, as it is a creation of menacing

terror. The metaphor vivifies both fear and darkness. In the
following lines, those feelings are further intensified as
Octaviano approaches Mariene's bedroom:

> Pisando las negras sombras
> en el silencio nocturno
> de la noche, has penetrado
> el jardín. (487a, italics mine)

When El Tetrarca also enters, the small light on the scene,
instead of illuminating, seems rather to increase the pervasive
dark:

> Este es su cuarto, y en él
> una escasa luz, nocturno
> Lucero, que late horror
> en repetidos impulsos... (488a)

By means of this image, the 'humanized" light, like the
anthropomorphised night, creates a horrific atmosphere "beating
horror" like a human heart that can feel the approaching tragedy.

The dark images culminate in Mariene's death in absolute
darkness as the only candle lighting the scene is extinguished in
the fight between Octaviano and El Tetrarca. As Bruce Wardropper
has stated, "When a metaphor becomes a visible object on stage or
a visualizable object in the spectator's imagination /here, when
the darkness leads to blindness and death/ it pervades the whole
play; a dominant symbol of great importance to the plot and
action is created."[21] The darkness shows both the terror and
blindness of the characters who, ironically, kill Mariene, the
woman both men loved.

The technique described by Wardropper is precisely that used
most often by Calderón in the plays of the middle period. In El
médico de su honra, the medical imagery becomes visible on stage

in the bleeding scene; in El pintor de su deshonra, Don Juan Roca twice (once metaphorically and once in reality) paints his dishonor; in La vida es sueño, Segismundo awakens from a sleep to deliver his great monologue on the world and on dreams. In this play, just as images of darkness are realized on stage, so too are there not one but several monsters that populate this world.[22]

Another aspect of nature that has a profound effect on the characters in El mayor monstruo del mundo is the sea. First El Tetrarca's armada sent against Octaviano is lost not due to human error but rather:

> Enojáronse las ondas
> y el mar, Nemrod de los aires,
> montes puso sobre montes (416b)

Later when El Tetrarca tries to rid himself of the dagger, which according to the prophecy, will kill Mariene, he throws it into the sea from where it returns imbedded in Tolomeo's back (461a). For the latter character, the sea is a "monumento inconstante" and for El Tetrarca it becomes a tomb since he commits suicide by throwing himself into the sea. The sea, surrounding the land whereon this play takes place, is organic to the action much of which takes place on the sea or near its shores. Sea imagery naturally arises from the context as it becomes both a comment on the ambience and on the destinies of the characters. With the stars, the sun, and the heavens, that the natural, cosmic imagery prepares the approaching tragedy as it slowly crushes the major characters.

The portentous natural surroundings are populated by frightening animals: asps, beasts, and vipers. Also some things are described in animalistic, terms. Antonio's ship is a "pez sin escama" and an "ave sin pluma" (464a); the river is "ese bruto cristalino...y música sus bramidos" (466a); El Tetrarca's letter to Tolomeo is "áspid y veneno" (477a) and once torn by Mariene, "una víbora... / que dividida en mitades, / con la lengua y la cola hiere" (478a). Finally, in El Tetrarca's impassioned speech about jealousy he portrays "los celos" as having:

> de sirena el canto,
> y de cocodrilo el llanto.
> de basilisco los ojos,
> los oídos, para enojos,
> del áspid... (485a)

The characters find themselves in an unhinged world where both nature and inanimate objects threaten their lives. Even in the few passages where a beautiful and peaceful nature is described, these harmonious pictures only contrast with the person in that atmosphere:

> Hermosa Mariene,
> a quien el orbe de zafir previene
> ya soberano asiento,
> como estrella añadida al firmamento:
> no con tanta tristeza
> turbes el rosicler de tu belleza. (458a)

The correspondences between the ugly, monstrous nature and fear, jealousy, sadness, suspicion, and egotism in the characters are well delineated. In this topsy turvy world, neither the few peaceful animals nor references to a potentially peaceful nature can influence the destinies of the characters. Nature is a force in the organic development of the play and it seems hardly sufficient to talk about the "atmosphere" created by these images. For here, nature is not "background" nor is it possible to disjoin nature from character, theme, or structure in this play or, in fact, from most of the works of the middle period.

Nature is an integral, inseparable feature of these comedias, especially since man and nature are in a continuous relationship throughout the works.

This violent nature becomes a prison for the characters in El mayor monstruo del mundo. We have already seen how El Tetrarca's ships are surrounded, imprisoned, and finally destroyed by the waves. The sea is also El Tetrarca's tomb, and before, Mariene had also threatened to throw herself into the sea (484b). But even those images that, as the play opened, seemed so beautiful "orbe de cristal" (460b)," cristalino globo" (483b), "círculos de nieve" (459a), seen from another angle, underscore a static, paralyzed, cold cosmos (which may be compared also with savage nature -- indifference versus violence).

Within this paradigm of imprisoning images, even characters' actions become as suggestive as the metaphors they employ. A.A. Parker has shown the evolution from action to image and from image to action, "desde metáforas preñadas de ideas que iluminan los temas, a metáforas que se hacen símbolos, luego a símbolos que se encarnan en los mismos personajes."[23] In each act of the play, someone is held captive in a prison. In the first act, Malacuca is imprisoned for saying he is Aristóbolo; in the second, El Tetrarca is jailed for attempting to assassinate Octaviano; and in the third, Mariene encarcerates herself to avoid and punish her husband. From the literal prison to the spiritual one is but a short step.

Throughout the work, to reinforce the prison motif, there are constant references to towers, labyrinths, tombs, and jails. For example, Mariene has enclosed herself in her room as the play approaches its denouement, but from this literal imprisoning, the imagery takes a much more personal turn. Her clothes, for example, denote separation, encarceration, and death; she wears a dark veil,

siempre delante del rostro,

> que estorbará el que te vea
> siendo mis reales adornos
> eternamente este luto (484b)

The prison motif is intertwined with the images of darkness, and also the adjectives of time suggest eternity and thus prefigure her approaching death. When the maid helps her undress for bed, she speaks of loosening "el cabello / de las prisiones de día" (487a). The prison is closing in about her.

In the final scene, the confining imagery is everpresent. Not only is Mariene in an enclosed room but also in the next to last scene, she finds herself with Octaviano on one side and El Tetrarca on the other. She says that she is "entre dos peligros juntos, / entre dos muertes vecinas" (489a). At the same time, El Tetrarca tells her that he "será muro" of her honor and Octaviano says that he "será escudo" of her life. As the two men approach each other, Mariene is trapped between them, between two walls that close in on her.

All of the prison images, in turn, signal the concept of life held by the major figures: life is a trap from which there is no escape except death. None of the characters can avoid his or her destiny but then when Mariene accepted the prophecy at the beginning of the action, the trap began to close; for she had there denied herself the use of her free will. The trajectory of the images has been from the cosmic "orbe de cristal," "círculos de nieve" in the first act to a more reduced scale in the second, "torre," "sepulcro," "prisión," to the most personal and intimate in the third, "cuarto," "velo," "pecho/muro," "pecho/escudo." The development of the imagery in turn illuminates the development of the action: when the possibilities of escape are diminished, the image contracts accordingly to reflect the lack of viable alternatives. The central prison image varies until there is an entire cluster of words that suggest the same idea but from differing perspectives.

The audience, thus, has been able to distinguish degrees of metaphorical expression from the most obvious to the most indirect yet all of these images contribute to the overall tone, atmosphere, and thematic development.

Besides demonstrating the imprisoned life of the characters, there is another image pattern that suggests that the entire world of the play is out of joint. The poisonous and unnatural creatures of the surrounding world abound and that very world is indifferent and claustrophobic. Furthermore, the people live and move in the darkness of towers and prisons. To accentuate this atmosphere of entrapment and, indeed, of chaos, there are a series of wars fought between Octaviano and Herodes, between Octaviano and Antonio, and between Octaviano and Aristóbolo. On a smaller scale, the audience sees fights between Octaviano and El Tetrarca and between the latter and Mariene. There are also assassination attempts, suicides, death sentences, and murder, as well as the ominous presence of the dagger.

The people who must exist in such a world often speak of barbarism and madness, "otra pena, otro dolor," exclaims El Tetrarca in a passage on jealousy:

> otro tormento, otra ansia
> en el corazón no llevo...
> Sea barbaridad, sea
> locura, sea inconstancia,
> sea desesperación,
> sea frenesí, sea rabia,
> sea ira, sea letargo... (474b)

Mariene, upon hearing that her husband has plotted her death, describes him as worse than the most barbaric aspects of nature:

> Mas tú, más que todos fiero;
> mas tú, más bruto que todos,

            mas tú, bárbaro en fin,
            no sólo amparas, no sólo
            favoreces lo que amas,
            pero avaro de los gozos
            aun muriendo no los dejas (434a)

This very inhumanity was prefigured in the prophecy that foretold that El Tetrarca would kill what he most loved. Man is even more horrid than the frightening nature that surrounds him in this play.

    Not even love can save the characters because it is an idolatrous love[24] and the characters themselves admit its dreadful nature:

            Tetrarca: cuando amor no es locura
                    no es amor (462b)

            Aristóbolo: pues en rigor
                    no hay áspid como el amor (464b)

            Tetrarca: el mayor monstruo del mundo
                    que te amenaza a prodigios,
                    es mi amor (467a)

This terrifying atmosphere engenders a whole gamut of monsters and the imagery, thus, is organic, dramatically organic, for there exists an unbreakable bond between the atmosphere and the image. By means of the broad, linked image patterns the audience forsees the disaster awaiting the characters from the first minutes of the play. The patterns of images produce a claustrophobic atmosphere which encloses and isolates the characters in their circumscribed world.

Calderón is now thinking in patterns and no longer is there any disparity whatever between image and atmosphere. All of the inner organisms of the play are related through these large and encompassing patterns. The single image illuminates the pattern to which it belongs as it also emphasizes character, structure, and theme within the entire complex of the work. Disorder is reflected in the horrid aspects of nature which, along with other constituent elements, imprisons and inhibits the people who live in such an environment: they are prisoners of their world concept, and thus of their own minds.[25]

El médico de su honra

From the very first moments of El médico de su honra (1635) there is little doubt in the audience's mind that it is in a tragic world. The title itself suggests immediately that the matters to be dealt with in this work are of the greatest consequence: life, death, honor.[26] In addition, the first two sets of action have portentous overtones: Enrique falls from his horse, Pedro abandons him, Arias comments on the King's "fiera condición"[27]. Then there is the reunion of old lovers with Enrique still the ardent pursuer in spite of the fact that Mencía is now a married lady who, in her speeches, portrays herself as torn between honor and love.

Calderón establishes the tone of foreboding in the first moments of the play. Besides the ominous events themselves, the words in which they are expressed promise a tragic outcome. "¡Qué desdicha!, ¡Qué dolor!" (317a) exclaim Arias and Diego at Enrique's fall. Though Pedro hurries off, he decries the "horror y mancilla" of the Prince's fall.. Arias brands Pedro's leaving an action of a beastly and brutal man because as he implies by means of a vivid image, his half-brother, Enrique may be near death, "tropezando... / en los brazos de la muerte" (317b). Meanwhile, Mencía, who from her home sees Enrique's fall, describes the "gran desdicha" (318a). Desdicha appears twice more and references to death and blood are added to emphasize the frightening tone.

From these rapidly moving external events, things take a turn inward as both Mencía and Enrique, in their first confrontation, examine their past and present feelings. Calderón sees to it that there is no relief from the fear and tension thus far created. Words that will be key to the rest of the play have appeared, sangre, muerte, mirar, and in rapid succession so do others. Mencía demands silencio from Arias; she is torn between honor y amor; she is concerned with Enrique's salud; and Enrique declares his celos and his fears of death.

All of this is reduced, in an admirable concision, to few more than three hundred lines

The tragic, danger-filled tone is maintained throughout the play not only by the central images, but also by a varied yet unified vocabulary, varied in the sense that the word choice is rich, and unified in the sense that these words converge to produce the dramatic tone. For example, the dangerous atmosphere is augmented by the repetition of such words as honor (61 times), muerte (30), alma (29), celos (23), sangre (23), temor (14), variations on matar (17) and morir (14); muerta (3), muerto (6), acero (8), daga (11), and espada (6). In addition, the sadness that fills the play is underlined by a particular vocabulary also: mal, (27), triste (13), desdicha (12), agravio (12), dolor (10), pena (10), rigor (9), agravios (9), daño (9), ausencia (8), quejas (8), prisión (7), cruel (7), penas (6), tristeza (6), and turbado (6).

In this play, words from the above list are used on the average of about once every eight lines. The vocabulary of danger, however, is more clustered around certain moments of tension and not so evenly spread throughout the action as are the words of sadness. Also there is definitely a process of association at work in the passages as, for example, honor and muerte are found early on in close proximity (327, 335, 337) and later muerte and sangre (341, 345, 346-48). There is a trajectory of usage that can be plotted for certain words and images and the most effective character in whom to see this evolution is Don Gutierre.

One thing needs to be made clear at once: Gutierre, throughout the first act of the play, loves and trusts his wife absolutely. He does not understand the ambiguous language used by both Mencía and Enrique in their conversation about the Prince's "amigo" and he accepts the story at face value. In Gutierre's talk with Mencía, there is nothing in his vocabulary nor in his imagery to suggest anything but love and respect. He addresses her as his "bellísimo dueñc" and swears to the union of their souls, "a dos almas una vida, / dos vidas a un albedrío" (322b). Her love sustains him and he even asks her permission to go and meet the King. When she raises the question of jealousy over Leonor, he compares Leonor to a flame and Mencía to the sun and embellishes that comparison, like a truly ardent lover, by saying that a small star, Leonor, may seem beautiful until one has experienced the light, and warmth of the sun, Mencía[28]. Mencía is the focal point of his life. Even when the King later imprisons him, what Gutierre regrets most is not the King's anger, but "solo siento que hoy, / Mencía, no te he de ver" (327b). For Gutierre, in the first act, is that for him, love is no trifling matter. When he tries to excuse his actions with Leonor to the King, he declares:

> si amor y honor son pasiones
> del ánimo, a mi entender,
> quien hizo al amor ofensa,
> se le hace el honor en él;
> porque el agravio del gusto
> al alma toca también... (326b)

Love and honor are intimately connected in Gutierre's mind.

Though the central images of blood, silence, death, night, and honor are used throughout the first act, they are not used in a meaningful pattern by Gutierre. He employs the sun image to describe Mencía and he does speak of his honor in the Leonor episode, but the power of such themes and images that will be seen in Acts II and III, is not found in Act I. Gutierre must undergo a crisis before his diction becomes poetically charged. All around him, nonetheless, the key words have been used by other characters, and it is as though from these seemingly random seeds, the imagery will take root in his soul and grow to tragic heights.

In Act II, the crisis occurs. Having received permission to visit his wife after being in prison, Gutierre returns home unexpectedly. Enrique, having come to visit Mencía, is forced to hide. Mencía tells Gutierre that there is a man in the house, puts out the light, and allows Enrique to escape. In his hurry to leave, the Prince drops his dagger and Gutierre finds it. All of the action occurs at night thereby providing a convenient entry for the light-dark imagery: "a oscuras entraré, ciego abismo del alma, la noche en sombra fría / su manto va recogiendo" (all quotes from Gutierre, emphasis added p. 331). As Gutierre prepares to return to prison, he goes to embrace his wife who, upon seeing the dagger under her husband's cloak, suffers a paroxism of fright and guilt. She prefigures her own horrid death, "Al verte así, presumía / que ya en mi sangre bañada, / hoy moría desangrada" (332a). Gutierre cannot understand her violent reaction but his suspicions are aroused and the capacity for suspicion is Gutierre's most terrible trait. He exits saying to himself, "¡Ay honor mucho tenemos / que hablar a solas los dos!" (332a).

Throughout Act I, Gutierre is an honest and forthright man. He refuses to lie to Pedro about why he left Leonor and he tells Mencía exactly how he feels about both her and Leonor. He does not understand the ambiguities in the conversation between his wife and the Prince, yet when his suspicions are aroused, he both lies and resorts easily to linguistic ambiguity to hint at his anger. He tells Mencía that after searching the entire house he has found no trace of a man, after which he exclaims to himself, "Mas es engaño, ¡ay de mí / que esta daga que hallé, ¡cielos!, / con sospechas y recelos / previene mi muerte en sí" (331b). Furthermore, when he later notes that the design on the dagger that he found matches that on Enrique's sword, he ambiguously threatens the Prince in the "Sois fuerte enemigo vos" speech (334a). Even Enrique recognizes that Gutierre is upset, "De sus

/Gutierre's7 quejas y suspiros / grandes sospechas prevengo"
(334a).

Gutierre has changed and when he is once more alone, he
develops the central conceit of the play. But, this conceit does
not spring into his mind from the void, as it were, it has been
carefully prepared since the first act. When he first met the
Prince, Gutierre knew that Enrique had fallen from his horse and
his speech reflects true concern for the nobleman's health.
Gutierre's attitude shows his anxiety when talking about the
Prince's fall, as well as when he expresses his sadness due to
the accident, his true hope for a quick recovery and concern for
the Prince's "salud" (320-21).[29] We have already noted his
concern with honor as well as his famed suspiciousness. Mencía
too mentioned blood and death when she saw the dagger under
Gutierre's cloak. Those elements plus the previous mentions of
darkness, light, love, and discretion all come to fruition in
his powerful monologue (334-35).

Gutierre's speech recapitulates all of the events leading up
to this moment of decision and predicts the moves that he will
make from now on. To decide rationally how to proceed, he must
constantly wage war against his own passions. He begins, "Ya
estoy solo, ya bien puedo / hablar" but his first words deny the
possibility of succinctly stating his fear, anger, and
frustration. The anaphora as well as the parallel construction
that characterize this part of the speech rhetorically reinforce
his pain and anguish:

> tantos géneros de agravios,
> tantos linajes de penas,
> como cobardes me asaltan,
> como atrevidos me cercan...

He calls on his valor and asks for justice for his honor as he
again tries to quash his feelings, "Pero cese el sentimiento, /

Pero vengamos al caso, / quizá hallaremos la respuesta." We see
the incessant battle raging within this character, a battle
between logic and emotion. He searches for an answer and cries
out, "¡Oh ruego a Dios que la haya! / ¡Oh plegue a Dios que la
tenga!"

Gutierre reviews the events of the past night and cannot
decide whether or not Mencía is guilty of complicity in the
Prince's visit. At this point, however, he has exhausted his
reasons and as discursive logic fails, dramatic imagery surges
forth. Gutierre has reached a moment when he must act. He
compares Mencía to the sun in its purity and beauty, as on 322,
but now the sun can be eclipsed by "una nube negra." He admits
the threat to his honor as well as his doubts while images of
darkness, death, and danger appear with ever increasing
frequency: turbar, manchar, eclipsar, helar, morir, padecer
peligro, sepulcro (334b).

Because of his past contact with medical vocabulary used by
others and by himself, and because of the danger that he feels
his honor to be in, he conceives of his honor as a patient in
need of care and he will provide that care as "médico de honor."
He will continue, as much as possible, to exercise self-control,
to watch his wife closely, to treat her well -- in other words,
to continue the deception that he has already begun to practice.
And, though Gutierre uses such words as accidente, agravios,
celos, dolor, etc..., he never mentions "blood."

Sangre appears in an explosion of anger at the end of Act II
and grows in prominence until it becomes one of the most frequent
words in Gutierre's vocabulary. When Mencía mistakes Gutierre
for Enrique in the garden scene, he can scarcely control his
rage. As Gutierre momentarily loses control he says that if he
ever were truly jealous, he would be capable of ripping out a
heart and eating it, adding, "a bocados la sangre me bebiera"
(388b). But even here he has not decided to kill Mencía nor has
the idea of bleeding her to death occurred to him. Gutierre must

undergo two more crises before he is moved to perform the final bloody act.

The first of these events is the interview between the King and his brother. Before the meeting, Gutierre told Pedro that the Prince had compromised his honor and that the offense can only be cleansed by the shedding of blood. He hastens to add, however, "con sangre digo / solamente de mi pecho" (339b). The statement is rather more ominous than it seems since, as Wardropper has shown, "At the wedding /of Gutierre and Mencía7 two fleshes have become sacramentally one; since in the honor play this single flesh has been diseased, the only recourse open to the man -- the 'head' of the union -- is to amputate."[30]

As Pedro confronts Enrique with this information, the blood references grow in number. He tells his wayward brother that the dagger could have become stained with the Prince's own blood, "mancharse con sangre vuestra" (341a all italics mine). As Pedro hands Enrique the dagger, the Prince accidentally cuts his brother's hand, "tu acero en mi sangre tiñes" (341a) and Enrique cannot believe that Pedro can accuse him of intentional harm, "no imagines / que puedo verter tu sangre" (341b). Pedro, like Mencía before him, prefigures his own death, "Bañado me vi en mi sangre" (341b). When Gutierre picks up the dropped dagger, perhaps because of Pedro's precisely parallel statement to Mencía's "en mi sangre bañada, / hoy noría desangrada" (332a), he decides that with very dagger, she must die, "con él muera" (341b).

The final episode that decides the manner of Mencía's death begins when Gutierre finds her writing a letter to the departing Enrique. He renews his use of medical imagery, returning to the original conceit, "Ya que la cura he de aplicar postrera, / no muera el alma, aunque la vida" (343b -- he will permit her time for confession before her death.

The blood imagery is constant in the last scenes of the play occurring in one form or another 17 times: sangre, sangría,

sangrarse, sangrienta(o), sangróse, sangrarla, desangrada. The
verbal imagery is triply underscored by the subsequent visual
impact of Mencía's body on stage "desangrada", by the blood
stains on the door of Gutierre's house, and by the bloody hand
given in marriage in the final scene.

The trajectory of the development of the imagery, in which
four stages are identifiable, can be now understood. First,
there is a preliminary stage where a particular set of words are
used because a particular situation brings them out -- Enrique's
fall creates doubt about his life and health, and his blood is
mentioned. Second, the word sangre is used metaphorically to
refer to family and lineage or it is used in other set phrases.
Third, blood is spoken of in a moment of high tension and then
related by Gutierre to the central conceit, forming, in the
process, a tight link, blood/médico de honor. And finally, from
the cumulative effect of the imagery grows the action when
Gutierre has Mencía bled to death. There is also a
distinguishable process of internalization at work. Gutierre
hears words used in his presence that do not seem to make a great
impact on him, but as he passes from crisis to crisis, his
vocabulary becomes focused precisely on these words he heard
earlier. As he internalizes the vocabulary and makes it his own,
he becomes a metaphorical physician who treats the disease.[31]

Gutierre acts on the basis of what he sees and hears. The
audience knows that he does not understand the whole truth about
Mencía, and largely from this gap comes the tension in the play.
Gutierre proceeds logically, as he sees it, but his logic is
based on false, or partially false, premises. He constantly
debates what sort of action to take, as though he himself were
aware of possible errors, and his hesitancy is reflected in his
language, in his use of "if/then" phrases. Gutierre's use of
these phrases does not begin until near the end of Act I, and
they occur in moments of doubt and tension. A relationship
between the rise of these phrases and the rise of the blood

imagery can be posited. "If" Gutierre says, "si amor y honor son pasiones / del ánimo... / quien hizo al amor ofensa, / se le hace el honor en él" (326b). This first occurrence of the if/then phrases sets up a situation which is key to Gutierre's feelings throughout the play and here it is linked with his actions regarding Leonor. Later, questioning himself about his feelings of jealousy, he adds, "que si es ponzoña que engendra / mi pecho, si no me dio / la muerte ¡Ay de mi!) al verterla / al volverla a mí podrá" (335a). Or rather, if it is really jealousy, then when fully acknowledged, it could cause death. In his subsequent angry outburst, he claims that if he were hurt, he would be capable of destroying Mencía (338b).

In the final act, a cold, calculating logic takes over as he says "¿Sí aquí le /a Mencía/ doy la muerte...? / Mas esto ha de pensarse de otra suerte" (343b). He tells Ludovico to obey "si quieres / vivir" (345a), and he adds that no one can accuse him of murder "si es posible / que una venda se desate" (345a). Yet, for all of his effort at logic, he is caught and the King tells him that he must now marry Leonor. Gutierre, not having learned his lesson, reverts to a series of "if" questions with the King now providing the "then" responses:

>   ¿Si vuelvo a verme
>   en desdichas tan extrañas,
>   que de noche halle esbozado
>   a vuestro hermano en mi casa?

Rey: No dar crédito a sospechas.
and the most dramatic one:

>   ¿Y si volviendo a mi casa
>   hallo algún papel que pide
>   que el Infante no se vaya?
> Rey: Para todo habrá remedio.

```
Gut:   ¿Posible es que a esto le haya?
Rey:   Sí Gutierre
Gut:              ¿Cuál señor?
Rey:   Uno vuestro.
Gut:            ¿Qué es?
Rey:                      Sangrarla.
```

El medico de su honra shows how characterization changes course by means of language as the character moves from a state of happiness through a series of crises leading to a tragic denouement. This play is, in part, another in a series that investigates the consequences of man's limited knowledge. As Manuel in La dama duende attempted to reason out the riddle based on evidence he gathered through his senses, so too does Gutierre try to verify his wife's supposed infidelity through investigation. He, like Manuel, trusts altogether too much in what he sees and hears, but in this play, the outcome and the atmosphere are all too tragic. The question of the limits of man's knowledge is one that Calderón treats in many plays like these two and in La vida es sueño, to cite only one more example.

Don Gutierre, trusting as he does in his senses, is bound to be affected by what is said around him. From random words said by others, he selects those that most appeal to him in his moments of tension and crisis. He uses images when normal discourse fails adequately to portray his inner anguish. From the imagery grows the horrid act with which this drama concludes. Just as Gutierre is a prisoner of the system in which he lives, so too is he a prisoner of the language he uses.

La vida es sueño

More has been written about La vida es sueño than about any other play by Calderón. In part, this is due to the philosophical meanings in the work, in part, to its structure, and in part, to its style. Three of the most important critical statements on the principal image patterns need to be briefly summarized before turning to another central 'verbal' aspect of the play.

The dream imagery has been brilliantly explicated by E.M. Wilson in an article that analyzes the meaning of "dream" and contrasts it with awakening to life.[32] In dreams, passions rule our actions and we do not act but instead are acted upon. Thus, a man who is subject to his passions, who does not try to govern his actions through reason, is living a dream rather than a meaningful life. When Segismundo awakens in the cave after his experience in the palace, he believes that what he had felt was real is now unreal and thus must have been a dream. When Clotaldo adds: "Que aun en sueños / no se pierde el hacer bien", Segismundo agrees. But, there is a logical fault here, as Wilson says, since in dreams, man cannot control his actions. Segismundo, however, seems to grasp that if he had tried to curb his instincts, the palace dream might have continued and future disappointments might have been avoided. Segismundo's decision here is not based on the highest of motives, and his real conversion will occur in the last act. Then, he realizes that death is an awakening from life which is a dream and once he has seen that "all life as the worldly know it" is a dream, he understands that one dreams, not that one is, but rather what one is. Thus it is within our power to change those things that can be changed; to use our abilities for good rather than for personal gain; and to accept those things over which we have no control. Man must learn to exercise both his reason and his free will and to make choices wisely.

In his article, "Some Observations on Imagery in 'La vida es sueño'",[33] Everett Hesse notes, there is an abundance of imagery in the first act and less imagery as the play progresses. Since the imagery mirrors "the emotional upheaval of the main characters" (421) and since Segismundo becomes more and more rational as he succeeds in controlling his passions, this kind of progression in the play reflects the action quite precisely. Hesse then gives us a catalogue of the major images and their meanings. The horse represents speed, violence, and emotional imbalance as it suggests Rosaura's "impetuosity and headlong dash for vengeance" (422). The rider, then, can be the controlling factor and represent reason. The eagle suggests the grandeur and majesty of the king and serves to introduce Segismundo into his possible future role. The man-beast images warn of the battle raging within Segismundo's breast as he learns to control his instincts by reason. Many of the buildings refer to the "lair of the beast" (424) and to the darkness of living death (the tower). Wild underbrush and general chaos in Nature reflect chaos in the characters. Light symbolizes reason and "redeemable humanity" (427) as well as love and truth (428). Hesse concludes by accentuating the visual nature of the images and suggesting that they offer vivid mental pictures to the audience. In addition the images are indicators of the more abstract meanings related to the main themes and to the overall significance of the play.

Margaret Maurin has recently shown the function of the interrelated patterns of the monster, sepulchre, and dark images.[34] Rosaura's horse, from which she falls at the beginning of the play, becomes a monster since it is totally alien to the human factor and since it is associated with the labyrinthine surroundings that predominate at the beginning of the play. But the monster image does not limit itself to only that scene and that circumstance as it becomes closely allied also to Segismundo himself. First, since he lives in the wild setting where the horse stumbled, in the labyrinth, he must also be a monster.

Second, Segismundo, through a transformation of the bull image, compares himself to the beast. Third, before his birth, Clorilene dreamed that she would give life to "Un monstruo en forma de hombre" and Basilio declared that he felt compelled to incarcerate "la fiera que había nacido." The rationale underlying the comparison is that of the passions overruling the rational aspects of man; Segismundo, like an animal, is governed by his appetites (134-37).

The death-sepulchre images are related to the idea of the living dead. Rosaura, for instance, has been dishonored and is thus "dead" though physically alive. These images can also be compared to events that are contrary to nature, for example, Segismundo was born with free will, but since he was imprisoned, he was denied his rights as a human being. He also is then "dead" though he is physically alive. Closely allied to these images is the use of chiaroscuro. Segismundo lives in a shadowy world, a world of darkness and of death, from which he can finally escape by following first the light that is Rosaura and his love for her, and second, the light of reason (139-44).

Yet another element in the verbal structure of the play has received less close attention despite the fact that many of the images are closely allied to it: word play. By "word play" we mean such things as puns, rhetorical figures like oxymoron and catachresis, sound play, and multiple verb forms. In the earlier plays, such items were a manner of clever entertainment or of quick repartee, but in the middle period, the multifaceted quality inherent in word play contributes to the themes and to an ambiguity that leads to a multiplicity of meaning quite common in the Baroque.[35] From ambiguity arise tensions caused by a disparity between what a character says, how other characters interpret his words, and how the audience, from its superior position, understands the statements.

In La vida es sueño, Clarín is the principal, but not the only, punster. His puns are clever and witty as when he plays on

Rosaura's expression of gratitude to Clotaldo for having saved her life: "Tus pies beso / mil veces," she declares, to which the gracioso adds, "Y yo los viso / que una letra más o menos / no reparan dos amigos" (509b). The pun shows a lively disrespect characteristic of the servant, but in Act II he puns on his own name with much more vicious undertones as he intimidates Clotaldo by threatening to reveal Rosaura's true identity, "...que soy Clarín / y que si el tal Clarín suena / podrá decir cuanto pasa / al Rey..." (512b). Not even jail can quash his humor as when he complains of hunger saying "en el filósofo leo / Nicomedes, y las noches / en el concilio Niceno" (523a). The pun is on the old form of ni coméis--nicomedes and on ni ceno. Finally, when he is mistaken by the soldiers for Segismundo, Clarín plays the role until he is found out. During this adventure, he wonders if this is perhaps how they treat everyone in this strange world in which he has entered, make them a prisoner one day and a prince the next. Clarín tells them that it is not his fault that they mistook him since, afterall, "vosotros fuisteis los que / me segismundasteis" (523b).

Such humor from a gracioso is the norm, but here two differences from earlier examples of the same character type can be discovered. [First, Clarín is a blackmailer and, therefore, more dangerous than other graciosos, who usually went only so far as to sisar from their masters.] Clarín threatens Clotaldo with revealing vital secrets. And second, the puns underscore his status as an hombre de burlas, a status that changes abruptly when he faces unexpected death. For it is Clarín, the comic character, who explains to Basilio that one must face life directly, something that neither Clarín nor the King has done before. "Mirad," he tells the sovereign, "que vais a morir / si está de Dios que muráis." (531b) His language now shows his transformed condition just as before his puns demonstrated his easy going, opportunistic life style which, in such a play as this, is doomed to failure.

In this drama, Calderón seems to delight in playing with the sound and forms of words:

> Pero, véate yo, y muera;
> que no sé, rendido ya,
> si el verte muerte me da,
> el no verte que me diera.
> Fuera más que muerte fiera,
> ira, rabia y dolor fuerte:
> fuera vida; desta suerte
> su rigor he ponderado,
> pues dar vida a un desdichado
> es dar a un dichoso muerte. (503b)

Figures of repetition were the stock and trade of the poets of this period and in this brief passage spoken by Segismundo, there are several: anaphora (fuera, fuera); polyptoton (repetition of words derived from the same root dar, da, diera); antimetabole (a logical conversion that turns about a sentence "dar vida a un desdichado / es dar a un dichoso muerte"); and the repetition of sounds as part of an internal rhyme pattern (verte, muerte, fuerte, suerte; muera, fuera; diera, fiera). We could, in fact, go through this play and come up with a veritable dictionary of rhetoric. While this rhetorical handbook might then show us how Calderón was taught to embellish his verse with tropes and figures, simply naming these figures does not demonstrate how they function dramatically or poetically. To quote M.M. Mahood, writing on a parallel feature in Shakespeare, "Naming the parts does not show us what makes the gun go off."[36]

Repetition, besides being pleasing to the ear, has the value of emphasizing ideas and themes by accentuating parallel or antithetical structure. Spoken aloud, as these verses were on stage, these repeated words and ideas gain extra value. In this passage, Segismundo lays repeated emphasis on seeing, on death,

and on suffering. He has just seen Rosaura for the first time
and her beauty has profoundly affected him. Her beauty, later
conceptualized on a Platonic level, will be one of the factors
responsible for his conversion from a man of the beasts to a man
of reason and self-control. Segismundo first threatens Rosaura
with death, then, after seeing how lovely she is, thinks of his
own death if he must part from her. In the play, Segismundo must
metaphorically die (be returned to the darkness of the cave)
before he can be reborn again and conquer his passions. Fury and
"dolor fuerte" also characterize Segismundo's "animal" stage
before his transformation. The Prince expresses his thoughts of
suffering as he begins to fall in love with Rosaura. The word
play in this selection is more than gratuitous wit; it emphasizes
the major themes of the play at this moment of "turbación" in
Segismundo's life for it is at this precise moment that he first
controls "esta fiera condición."

The final aspects of word play to be treated are the figures
in which there is an exchange of elements. E.M. Wilson in his
pioneering study of the four elements in the imagery of
Calderón,[37] states that this exchange shows confusion and, at
times, violent action. That is certainly true in La vida es
sueño wherein these figures constantly appear. But, as Wilson
himself points out, all of the plays in which this type of
imagery appear were "written for a separate performance, not to
make up a collected edition" (205). And, while they do show
confusion, they may also illustrate the most profound issues of a
play. In this play, a bird is a "flor de pluma / o ramillete con
alas" or "clarines de plumas"; a fish is a "bajel de escamas"; a
stream becomes a "sierpe de plata"; a pistol, "áspid / de
metal"; trumpets, "aves de metal." But the paradoxical aspect
carries over to the descriptions of the characters, mainly of
Segismundo who is "esqueleto vivo, animado muerto, monstruo en
forma de hombre, víbora humana, monstruo humano, un compuesto de
hombre y fiera, hombre de las fieras / y una fiera de los

hombres." Could one not say that all of these seemingly contradictory descriptions point to every one of the characters? This confusion of elements borders on chaos, yet if a bird may be a winged bouquet or a feathered flower and if a man may be a beast, then cannot a woman be a man (as Rosaura is at the beginning of the play), a wise man a fool (Basilio), a fool a wise man (Clarín in the last scene), a prince a fettered prisoner, and life a dream?

One may venture the possibility that in these images of confusion and chaos, of the exchange of elements, is really a microcosmic view of the principal theme of the entire play. If our senses fail us, if we cannot distinguish a bird from a flower or a stream from a snake, then on what do we rely? Calderón's answer at the end of the play suggests it is love, friendship, "lo eterno", and good works.

La desdicha de la voz and No hay cosa
como callar

Both La desdicha de la voz (1639) and No hay cosa como
callar (1639) employ the standard comedic devices found in
earlier capa y espada plays: complex intrigues, mirror scenes,
disguise, hidden lovers, humorous servants, unexpected arrivals,
and peripatetic action. But in these "comedies" there is
something definitely amiss.

The light tone, the humor that was appreciated in La dama
duende and in Casa con dos puertas seems either missing or
forced. In the earlier plays, although characters were flirting
with danger, the consequences, even of sword play, were not so
serious that one really feared for their lives. Not so in the
two works at hand, for in La desdicha de la voz, Diego is wounded
so seriously as to require over a month to recuperate. In No hay
cosa como callar, a servant is severely wounded in a fight with a
nobleman. To add to the discomfort, the manner in which both
Diego and the servant are treated is ignoble and callous. In the
first case, Diego is attacked by two noblemen[38] (one may contrast
this action with Luis' decision in La dama duende to cease
fighting when his brother rushes to his side). In the second,
the servant's plight is all but forgotten in the last scenes of
the play and even though Barzoque tries to laugh that away, he
cannot help but note that each of the principal characters:

> a su negocio
> está solamente atento,
> olvidados de un criado
> que está herido... (1037b)

What's more, in La desdicha de la voz, Don Pedro twice attempts
to kill his sister and Doña Leonor is brutally jilted at the end
of the play. In No hay cosa como callar, Doña Leonor is raped
and both Luis and Marcela are unexpectedly (at least by them)
abandoned by their lovers in the final scene. The results of

these two later plays only partially fulfill the expectations of what may be termed traditional "comedy."

Part of the difficulty with these "problem" or "dark" comedies[39] is that in neither of them is there a clear-cut comic pointer. A comic pointer, like Doña Angela in La dama duende, is a "character who observes and comments or who manipulates and controls the action and thereby provides superior knowledge."[40] The comic pointer, then, creates the distance necessary for the audience to appreciate humorously the seemingly dangerous situations. When this figure appears in conjunction with such devices as disguise or secret passages, escape from danger or power over risk-taking is near at hand. Interest is heightened when that control appears to be in jeopardy, but then deliverance comes just in the nick of time, as one knew it would all along. In neither La desdicha de la voz nor in No hay cosa como callar is there anyone conspicuously in control of the situations.

Furthermore, in the earlier plays, language play and props added to the fun of the hairbreadth escapes. In La dama duende, Manuel's "chivalric" letter added moments of linguistic amusement. Also, Cosme's superstitious belief in witchcraft provided scenes of both linguistic and emotional contrast between himself and his master's cool, yet easily fooled, reason. In fact, the "devil" motif is part of the high humor of the play from the title on. In No hay cosa como callar, the devil motif returns, but here in a potentially much more serious way. Valbuena Briones, in his edition of the play, signals "la posibilidad de la venta del alma con objeto de conseguir a una dama." Barzoque says, as Don Juan discovers Leonor in his bedroom:

> ¿cuando ofreces el alma
> te la hallas en tu aposento
> en fe de que acepto
> la palabra del diablo?

> ...pacto
> ha sido explícito, es cierto. (1011a).

The motif has taken a weighty turn.

In <u>Casa</u> <u>con</u> <u>dos</u> <u>puertas</u>, the action revolves about the central prop of a house with two doors. This prop creates confusion, humor, and some frantic action. In <u>La</u> <u>desdicha</u> <u>de</u> <u>la</u> <u>voz</u>, it is Beatriz's voice that causes the frenetic entrances and exits as well as the heightened confusion, but it also creates a potentially deadly danger to her life as her brother, upon hearing her sing, rushes madly about trying to kill her. Beatriz's voice, something from which she cannot escape, is as treacherous as it is beautiful. Her voice, in fact, is a complex image in that it is both talked about by others and used by Beatriz to speak and sing. This combination points to a movement, fully realized in the last period, toward the actualization of images on stage. In the last plays, horses will be talked about and they will be seen running across stage, caves will be spoken of and the audience will see them in their primitive state and as they are transformed into beautiful palaces, characters will speak of nature and finally become part of that very nature. Here in <u>La</u> <u>desdicha</u> <u>de</u> <u>la</u> <u>voz</u>, the voice acting both as poetic image as well as a physically activated aspect of a character signals a development toward the more theatrical works of the final period.

Characters in all four plays resort to deceit and trickery at times. But when Angela lies, there is an ironic humor in her remarks since they are generally couched in half-truths. In <u>La</u> <u>desdicha</u> <u>de</u> <u>la</u> <u>voz</u>, Beatriz lies outright to her brother about knowing Don Juan (918b), as she later lies about having been out of the house. The lies are not funny, only expedient:

> Pues calla el que yo
> fuera de la casa he salido;

> que si el mentir es forzoso
> al decirle donde fui,
> mentir diciendo que aquí
> he estado, es menos dañoso. (925b)

Octavio, an old, noble, and venerated friend of distinguished families, also lies to his friends. He tells Leonor that Lucía (Beatriz in disguise) was raised in a convent, became ill, wishes to become a nun but lacks sufficient funds, and that she is a model of virtue (935a). He then tells Pedro that he does not know where Beatriz is when he is hiding her in his own home all along (942-44).

Similarly, in No hay cosa como callar, Don Juan shows himself to be egocentric and vulgar in his treatment of women. In La dama duende, Manuel, it is true, puts business before love, but one can at least appreciate his motives since they touch on his family honor. To the end, however, he is a staunch, though bewildered, defender of women. Don Juan's feelings about women are of a different kind altogether. Barzoque says of him, "Como en siendo cara nueva, / siempre es superior; que en ti / la mejor es la postrera" (1001a). Don Juan's own statements are even coarser:

> porque burlándome dellas ⌐de las mujeres⌐
> la que a mí me dura más,
> es la que menos me cuesta (1001a)

> Luis: Pues
> ¿qué medio hay para olvidar
> una hermosura?
> Juan: Alcanzar
> esa hermosura. Esta es
> la cura, don Luis, más cuerda:
> porque ¿quién tan importuna

> pasión tuvo que de una
> lograda ocasión se acuerda?
> ¿Por qué pensáis que Macías
> enamorado murió?
> Porque nunca consiguió. (1018a)

In the earlier plays, to point out another contrast, the principal characters undergo some kind of trial or suffering before they are permitted to resolve their problems and to marry. In those plays, however, the suffering, while sometimes bordering on the intolerable (as for example, Angela's captive existence in her brothers' house), is relieved by moments of respite, and also the suffering is not extraordinarily demeaning. In the later two plays, the heroines must undergo nearly total degradation before being restored.

Beatriz (La desdicha de la voz) must abandon her home and take refuge from her brother's rage in the house of a poor but kindly neighbor (931b). She is then led to believe that the man she loves is dead (931b) and that her brother is the killer (932a). Since she cannot return home, she must sell the few jewels she was wearing and with that money leave Madrid disguised in an "humilde vestido" (932a). She seeks refuge in Sevilla where she lives for a month in an inn as a virtual prisoner of her own fears. She looks to Octavio for help and he places her in Leonor's service as a criada. Beatriz has almost given up all:

> Ya no soy quien soy, fortuna,
> sino una humilde y sujeta
> mujer. Adiós vanidad,
> estimación y soberbia,
> que ya expirasteis en mí. (932a)

She even has to change the way she speaks, "que hasta el estilo
he de mudar" (936b). But she has not yet reached the bottom of
the decline for now Luquete, the wine-loving gracioso, makes a
pass at her:

> ¡Eso solo le faltaba
> a mi discurso afligido:
> que un pícaro se me atreva! (947b)

Though what happens to Beatriz in her long fall is
unquestionably painful and demeaning Leonor's sufferings (No hay
cosa como callar) are immeasurably more brutal. Her brother and
lover go off to war; her house catches fire; she must spend the
night in the home of a neighbor whom she does not know; she is
raped by an unknown assailant; she suffers for a month before she
can take any action; and she loses the one bit of proof about her
violator's identity she had before her fortunes begin to improve.
Whereas in La desdicha de la voz Beatriz's voice functioned as a
complex image, in No hay cosa como callar silence acts in a
similar fashion. For it is when Leonor speaks of her suffering
which must be born in silence without others knowing of her,
literally, unspeakable pain and humilliation that we feel the
silence in all its poetic power. Leonor suffers alone on stage
unable to utter to any but herself and the audience her mute
tragedy.

In addition to the more tragic events that befall the
characters, the themes in the latter plays also seem "weightier"
than in either of the earlier plays. La dama duende and Casa con
dos puertas both treat honor, to be sure, but that theme is
secondary to discovery and love. In the later works, the greater
questions of personal integrity and worth, of appearance and
reality in the world, of the nature of man, as it were, bother
the audience. These questions may not be adequately answered in
these plays nor, for that matter, in the great honor plays of the

same period, but they are there and must be considered by the audience. Leonor's final long speech will demonstrate how different in tone is this play when compared to even Angela's confessional speech at the end of La dama duende :

> La vida vuestra y mi honor
> en dos balanzas a un tiempo
> puestas están. Pues yo miro
> por vuestra vida en tal riesgo,
> mirad por el honor mío
> vos igualmente...
> que soy mujer, finalmente,
> que moriré de un secreto,
> por no vivir de una voz;
> que en fin hablar no es remedio.
> vida y honor me debéis. (1035a)

The balance between life and honor and their implicit counterparts of death and dishonor are surely more profound and far-reaching than the confession of a love achieved through disguise and ingenious tricks, no matter how deep is that love.

In these later plays, then, an array of disturbing questions about what earlier were conventionally accepted noble characters involved in humorous love-triangles are presented. These later characters are deflated and degraded systematically before the required resolution in marriage provides an escape. But even here, the marriages, the final outcome, are less than satisfactory for many of the "loose threads" remain untied.

These plays, like others in this period, involve us in discoveries. The revelations are not, however, just those of the identity of unknown lovers, but rather of an evil reality that lies beneath the fair, courtly appearances of these noble men and women. These discoveries are painful and the audience is made to feel the pain of abandonment, violation, physical harm, fall from

position all created by chance circumstance and mean trickery.
The actualized image complexes of voice and silence make us
participate vividly in the heroines' trials . Beatriz suffers
ignominies before she decides to cast her fate, out of simple
hope for any better situation, with her lover, and Leonor is
violated when Don Juan finds her in his room. His decision to
marry her is made under pressure and is undertaken more out of
fear of dishonor than out of any sense of love or desire. Both
these plays cut deeply enough to be tragic even though they are
played out with the techniques of comedy. Instead of laughing at
the unexpected discovery, we wince in momentary pain since the
revelation leads inevitably to greater anguish. The imagery is
becoming more complex, theatrical, and personal to both the
characters and the audience. Something has happened in
Calderón's theater. The greater questions about man are
influencing his dramas of the 1630-1650 period and though he
attempts to write comedies, his uneasiness, shown also in La vida
es sueño and in the three honor plays, is ever-present in these
"dark" comedies.

El pintor de su deshonra

El pintor de su deshonra is one of the most artistically
complex dramas in Calderón's production.[41] In this work,
Calderón masterfully orchestrates the themes of honor, love,
vengeance, art, music, time, and the sea, all set in a cosmic
background made up of the four elements, with water and earth as
the principal ones. At the same time he simultaneously explores
the consequences of a May-December marriage and the reunion of
old lovers. He employs a humorous gracioso who also functions as
a Greek chorus; he delves into the depths of the unconscious
mind; he scrutinizes the limits of friendship; he examines
tragedy and the "common responsibility in the final denouement of
all those who take part";[42] and he integrates all of these
elements into one superbly written drama. And, while El pintor
is the culmination of the techniques that characterize the dramas
of the 1630-1650 period, it also predicts the direction that the
last plays will take,

The discussion will focus primarily on three features of this
work: on the sea, art, and music, and how these themes are woven
into the complex web formed by other themes and images.

The fact that the action of this play takes place in Gaeta,
Barcelona, and Naples is not casual. These cities are near the
sea and the sea is a constant presence that must be dealt with by
all of the characters here as was the case with El mayor monstruo
del mundo. Luis is presumed by all to have been lost at sea.
Later he not only returns to the sea, but also kidnaps Serafina
and runs from his pursuers to the sea. Juan and Serafina live
near the ocean, and when Serafina is kidnapped, Juan throws
himself into the sea in pursuit. Serafina is called a sirena
(889b), a fijo escollo who withstands the "embates continuos /
del mar" (882b), which are, in turn, a metaphor for Alvaro's
unwanted constancy. Alvaro disguises himself as a marinero to be
later termed Pirata by both Don Juan and by his own father (891b
and 892a).

It was the sea, "esa azul campaña" (869b) that took Alvaro away in the first place and in a great storm at sea he was presumed lost. It is likewise the sea that brings him home, and his homecoming causes the first of the omens, in this case, shots, that are heard throughout the play: "Disparan dentro... / La atalaya ha descubierto / de Nápoles dos galeras, / que, costeando sus riberas, / vienen ya tomando puerto" (871b). The sea provides his escape after he has captured Serafina, "¿En mis brazos Serafina / no está ya? ¿No está en la playa / aguardando un bergantín? / Pues ¿qué espera, pues qué aguarda / mi amor? Amigos al mar" (890b). Don Juan attempts to rescue his wife as he throws himself into the sea to become, according to the bystanders, a "racional barca" (891b).

Besides these key moments, the sea imagery pervades other moments of the play as for example the fact that a family's business is routinely carried out by sea. The sea even enters the love imagery as Don Juan calls his wife "Venus de este mar" (869a) and love's sting is likened to a "severo arpón." (886a, 887a). The Prince's love for Serafina is compared to a small fountain that is born near the sea, "orilla / del mar" (885b). The most beautiful site in Barcelona, according to Don Juan, is Don Diego de Cardona's home "porque es / sobre el mar" (883b) and the violence of the fire that occurs at that very home is thus similar to a "volcán del mar" (890b).

The violence of the sea, in fact, is one of the aspects of this subject that infuses most of the major scenes in the first two acts. The main representative of the destructive aspects of the sea is Don Alvaro, while both Serafina and Don Juan are mere pawns moved about by the actions of the rash young man. The sea also suggests travel, an ebb and flow, and the comings and goings of the characters reaches mythic proportions in this work as Serafina's kidnapping is compared to the myth of the kidnapping of Deyanira by the half-man, half-beast (violent and lustful) Centaur.

As the peregrinations, willed and unwilled, of the major characters is shown in the image of the sea carrying them away or returning them to the shore, so also time, cyclical time, is a major factor in the development of the plot. Words that suggest the passage of time are ever present: años, mes, día, hora, momento, instante, etc..., as well as the iterative use of words that echo with the cyclical nature of time: cuna-sepulcro, nacer-morir, hoy-ayer. For example, Serafina's confessional speech to Porcia appeals to her friend's memory to recall "aquel venturoso tiempo" that was their youth when she loved and was loved by Don Alvaro. As she remembers her former lover, she faints only to awaken to find him before her. She says, "viuda de ti me he casado", thereby contrasting past with present and, later in the act, she denies the possibility of a future for the two of them, "que yo no he de amarte nunca." (879b).

The sea, consequently, not only is associated with Alvaro, but also serves to expand the dimensions of the action. Likewise two other central themes, art and music, portray certain characters, divide them into groups, and fuse with other themes and images.

Given the title of the play, the imagery of painting, appears abundantly throughout the work. As Alvaro was the main character allied to the sea, so Don Juan is the one most associated with painting since he is a painter by avocation and, because of a series of crises, becomes a "pintor de su deshonra." Serafina's very name alludes to her extraordinary beauty,[43] a beauty that Don Juan, despite his talent, cannot capture on canvas. He does have the ability, he tells us, to paint certain things with ease:

en una atención
imprime /la Naturaleza7 cualquier objeto
con más señas de un defeto,
mas bien, que una perfección;

y como sus partes son
más tratables, se asegura
la fealdad en la pintura;
y así con facilidad
se retrata una fealdad
primero que una hermosura (880a)

Calderón shows here not a failure of art, but the inadequacy of this particular man to imitate the beauty created by nature.[44] Juan Roca is able to paint his dishonor but even here, painting has undergone a change. Don Juan uses pistols, not brushes, and he paints in blood, not in oils. As he portrays the death scene he also paints the final desolation of both his own tragedy and that of his old friends, Don Luis and Don Pedro.

If painting is associated with honor, vengeance, and death, its positive counterpart is music. Music is allied to dance and the two become a metaphor for love: "Quien ve de lejos danzar / al que más airoso ha sido," the Prince explains to Celio who declares that he has never been in love:

como no oye el dulce ruido
de la música, en juzgar
que está loco, juzga bien,
pues sin compás las acciones
parecen desatenciones:
lo que no sucede a quien
de cerca oye la armonía,
que es alma de su primor. (376a)

To be in love, one must give oneself over to the "dulce ruido de la música." Love is a sweet madness that only lovers feel. Love is harmony and music whose concordance inflames the passions and makes the lover dance to its melodious sound.

The metaphorical passage is later presented visually in a choreographed scene that takes place in Porcia's garden. As she sings a song of love, the Prince approaches her balcony but, as the topic of the song changes to jealousy, he must go away. The change in topic is a signal to the Prince that the young lady's father is approaching. The Prince "dances" to the tune called by love.

Honor and love, allied to the painting and music/dance themes, are both called "tyrants." In his impassioned speech in the middle of Act III, Don Juan curses honor, "¡Mal haya el primero, amén, / que hizo ley tan rigurosa!" (897b) and then explains that honor is a social creation and a social tyrant which puts one man's reputation in the hands of others. Honor is an unnatural artifact created and upheld by society and by men like Juan who, at the same time that they rail against "este infame rito," sustain its practices. Love is also a tyrant, "Amor tirano" which can change men, but love's tyranny is an individual rule not subject to society's domination. Love happens and cannot be governed by will or reason. The Prince, for examples, falls in love with Serafina even as he is courting Porcia. He cannot help his feelings but he can govern his passion. This control, in fact, is what distinguishes him from Alvaro.

As painting uses brushes and colors, music and dance use harmony and song. The brushes are replaced by pistols and the oils by blood, "un cuadro es, / que ha dibujado con sangre / el pintor de su deshonra" (903b) declares Don Juan in the last scene, as he makes a post hoc statement about their metaphorical transformation. Love too has its weapons "tanta flecha y tanto sol / tanta munición de rayos / y tanto severo arpón"(886a). But while love's arrows strike deep, they do not of themselves kill.

Another contrast is that music and dance are arts of movement while painting is static and spatial. All of the scenes wherein painting plays a part occur, framed, as it were, in enclosed areas, principally Don Juan's house and the little country building with its barred windows. The rooms form part of a larger prison motif from which there is finally no escape. The music-dance scenes, on the other hand, all take place in outdoors settings as, for example, in the garden near Porcia's home. These scenes are more closely allied to nature and sensuality than are the enclosures and prisons of painting.

Furthermore, painting and art are on several occasions suggestive of death. When Serafina, after being kidnapped, explains how she feels toward Alvaro, she compares herself to a lifeless statue:

> Tú, conseguida, no puedes
> conseguirme; pues es claro
> que no consigue quien no
> consigue el alma; y es llano
> que una hermosura sin ella
> es como estatua de mármol,
> en quien está la hermosura
> sin el color del halago,
> vencida, mas no gozada. (894a)

Conversely, dance and music are parallel to life in their variety, harmony, and fantasy.

In order better to see the relationships established thus far, a schematic diagram is provided below:

Music/Dance	Painting
Setting: open, gardens, outdoors	Setting: enclosed, houses, rooms, barred windows
Theme--Love	Theme--Honor
Natural tyrant	Social tyrant
Weapons--arrows	Weapons--pistols

Results--marriage, union   Results--death, isolation

This scheme would allow a division of the characters into two
groups: Prince, Porcia (music, dance,love, union) and Juan,
Serafina (painting, death, honor, isolation). In Calderón's
middle plays, however, such a black and white scheme is rarely
found.   In the early plays, a clearcut division was more often
the case, but in this play, there are two scenes wherein a
character from one group crosses over to the subject of the other
group. These scenes complicate matters and, therefore, we must
deal first with the dance scene between Serafina and Alvaro and
second with the painting scene in which the Prince takes a
role.must be treated separately.

     If, as has been suggested, dance and music are associated
with the positive aspects of love, though jealousy does enter in
a secondary way, then does not the scene between Serafina and
Alvaro in Act II ruin the scheme? Are there differences that we
can demonstrate in this scene that keep the plan intact while, at
the same time, developing certain contrasts that complicate yet
still suggest the already created design?

     The scene takes place at a festival in Barcelona where the
men have the right to ask any woman to dance and she must accept,
"ya es fuerza danzar" (888b), Don Juan tells his wife. Before
the start of the dance, however, Don Juan's suspicions have been
aroused when a man was discovered in his home. He still has his
doubts even though his wife has told him how happy she is to be
at the festival with him: "me atormento / con mi mismo
pensamiento" (888b), he confesses in an aside. The atmosphere
surrounding the dance, one of doubts, fears and questions about
honor, distinguishes this scene from other dance-music scenes.[45]

     Serafina only grudgingly agrees to dance because she
recognizes that it is Alvaro who has asked her.   In ambiguous
language she tries to discourage his offer. In her response, she
uses a dance term with which to couch her double meanings:

```
Don Alv:    ...¿queréis danzar
            conmigo?
Ser:                    Vuestra esperanza
            tarde pienso que llegó.
Don Alv:    ¿Por qué tarde?
Ser:                            Porque yo
            no estoy para hacer mudanza
            y es vana la pretensión vuestra. (888b)
```

In addition, unlike the other dance/music scenes, the participants here are masked; they hide their true identity and their purposes. Throughout the dance Serafina refers to Alvaro only as "Máscara" refusing even to say his name. According to the song, even Love is disguised:

```
Veniu las minonas
a bailar al Clos
¡Tararera!
que en las Carnestolendas
se disfraza Amor...
que en Carnestolendas
Amor se disfraz. (888a)
```

True, open, noble love is disfigured and lurking behind the mask is Alvaro's ignoble and dangerous passion. In this scene, true love is turned upside down and the whole emblematic quality of the music-dance theme is perverted so that the audience may contrast this moment with others in the play.

A similar subversion can be observed in the painting scene wherein the Prince plays a major role. Calderón has quite carefully laid the groundwork for the episode between Roca and the Prince. Though the two men met briefly in the first act, the Prince said that he did not really notice Don Juan:

                    No
    reparé entonces en él,
    como no le conocía;
    y aun otra vez si le viera,
    no sé si le conociera. (877a)

Besides, when the Prince does meet him again, Don Juan, like Don
Alvaro in the previously discussed scenes, is in disguise "con
vestido pobre" (897a).

    The Prince has been attracted to Serafina's great beauty
since he first saw her. But again Calderón has meticulously
sought to contrast the Prince's fascination with Alvaro's
insistent passion. Though he is drawn to Serafina, after
discovering that she is married, he states:

    Mas no imagino nada;
    que es necedad, que es locura
    idolatrar hermosura
    antes perdida que hallada. (877b)

When he is alone with her in Act III, he cannot help but hint at
the love he feels for her, yet when she asks him to guard the
fact that she is there in the mountains, he swears that "Vuestro
nombre / jamás saldrá de mi labio" and he leaves her alone.

    Though he leaves, he still loves Serafina and is determined
to have her portrait near him so that it may help relieve his
suffering. He commissions Don Juan to carry out the painting in
secret, still trying to be discreet. In their subsequent
conversation, language once more becomes double-edged as when Don
Juan tells the Prince, "que aunque un humilde pintor / soy,
quizá por ser honrado / vivo así" (899a), to which the Prince
responds with unintentional irony, "cree de mí que, agradecido /
verás tu deseo cumplido" (899a).

As before, the language is ambiguous and the tone is menacing. One of the characters, unbeknownst to others, is in disguise so that he may achieve his desires. Furthermore, as in the music-dance sequence, the atmosphere has been charged with danger previous to the discussion under scrutiny. Don Juan has just shown and described to the Prince the painting of the kidnapping of Deyanira so that all of the overtones of death, fire, and vengeance are vividly before the audience.[46] While the Prince hopes that the painting of Serafina will give him solace from the impossible love he feels, it will instead present him with a bloody death scene that shocks him to his senses, after which he immediately decides to marry Porcia, his true love.

There are so many more important elements that are linked to the music-dance and art themes that it is impossible to do justice in a brief space to their complex interweaving. Nevertheless, some of them can be quickly suggested: in the song in Act II one finds the religious imagery (ídolo, altar, imagen, templo) that is usually associated with Alvaro's idolatrous love of Serafina (see also 882b); in the Hercules painting is a powerful fire image which has been associated with Don Juan since Act II; the mask and disguise motif are linked to both painting and dance and to Alvaro and Don Juan, suggesting parallels between the two men; the "allegorical" nature of the Hercules painting could be easily tied to the same quality in Juanete's stories; the link between painting and the prison and music/dance and nature has only been hinted at throughout this discussion and could yield interesting relationships with a sterility (Don Juan), fertility (Prince) motif.

El pintor de su deshonra is unquestionably a tour de force in the superb blending of elements that make up the great image-theme plays of the 1630-1650 period. There are no wasted lines nor wasted scenes, as every word contributes to the inevitable denouement. Calderón has taken the honor theme in this play as far as it can go in presenting this most complex and desolate view. At the end of the play, the protagonist must now face life after having killed his wife and her lover, who are the children of his best friends. Unlike Gutierre of El médico de su honra, he has not the palest of opportunities for a new beginning,[47] and unlike Don Lope de Almeida of A secreto agravio, secreta venganza, he cannot go off to war to find relief in death. The isolation, the dark view of honor has reached the final pass beyond which it cannot go. Don Juan must live in misery and loneliness, though ironically "blessed" by society's pardon, for the rest of his life.[48]

Introduction to Part III

The last plays, coming as they do after the great honor
tragedies, and subsequent to the philosophical statement of La
vida es sueño as well as to the striking portrayal of realistic
characters in El alcalde de Zalamea, suffer from a chronological
disadvantage that becomes obvious as one peruses the criticism.

In the honor dramas, perhaps because of the tragic outcomes
they portray, a natural order prevails. Violations of natural
law provoke disorder until retribution is exacted from the
guilty, and order, at least temporarily, is restored. No totally
innocent person suffers a fall in these plays, though at times it
seems that the "poetic justice" visited on some of the characters
is not equal to their faults.

The dramatist sets up an ambience, a tone, from the first of
the middle plays through the observation of which an attentive
member of the audience can see from the outset that the play will
end in the death of one or more of the characters. In these
works, the audience must be convinced of a chain, an unbreakable
chain, of cause and effect that leads ineluctably to the foreseen
denouement. In short, the world of the play must more or less
mirror the real world of the audience. Our involvement depends
on dramatic probability. A.A. Parker has made the same case, in
another form, by beginning at the end of the play and
discovering the threat that leads back to the first cause of the
final poetic justice. This logical development of cause and
effect is not always at work in the last plays.[49]

Since many of the last works take place in the mythological
world, the gods have the final word about the outcome of the
characters. At times, when an impasse is reached, a god or god-
figure will descend to the stage and resolve the difficulties --
see, for example, Apollo and Jupiter's role in El hijo del sol
Faetón, Casimiro's role in Hado y divisa de Leonido y Marfisa,
or Apollo in La estatua de Prometeo. Situations that seem to
lead inevitably to bloodshed are also changed at the last moment

by the intervention of a supernatural character who may be, at times, controlled by a magician -- see Lisipo and Megara's roles in Hado y divisa de Leonido y Marfisa. And, often, future events are shown on stage in one act, acted out again in a later act, and the events changed -- see En esta vida todo es verdad y todo mentira. In the final plays, the audience cannot rely absolutely on logic nor on what has previously been the normal cause and effect relationships seen in earlier works.

At the end of El pintor de su deshonra, a dark picture of general suffering is portrayed. This bleak view, despite the pardon of Don Juan Roca and the restoration of social order, gives way, in the myth plays and in the comedias novelescas of the final period, to another view. It seems as though with El pintor Calderón has reached the end of one path and has begun to seek out another. For in the last plays, death is not the final word. While it is true that characters do die, their deaths are rarely final. They are transformed into elements of nature or their deaths provide for the renewal of society and of the natural world.

Little has been written on either the myth plays or on the comedias novelescas and, in what has been written, the general tendency has been either to dismiss them as courtly spectacles of more show than substance or to attempt to see in the works some sort of allegorical statement. Part of the problem has been not examining the final works on their own artistic grounds. Looking for a sort of realism that was found in the middle plays will only lead to frustration and confusion. If one accepts the world that these plays attempt to portray, one may indeed be in awe of what one sees, but one does not find the events so improbable as to cause the action to be dismissed as totally unbelievable. If one refuses to enter the created world then, of course, the plays will appear to be absurd and no more than theatrical spectacles. The same thing applies, however, to the honor plays. If one rejects the frightening world, shown vividly by Calderón, in

which mere suspicions about honor can lead to murder, then these
plays too would be dismissed as absurd and bloody spectacles.

The style of the myth plays does not appear suddenly in
Calderón's career. In the early 1650s, moreover, he wrote plays
that harken back to the works of the middle period but yet point
ahead to the later plays. Once again, the transition is slow and
deliberate.

It is both easy and difficult to generalize about the
imagery in the last plays. Calderón still uses imagery to
underscore character, to emphasize his major themes, to control
tone and atmosphere, to help focus scene changes and, thereby, to
underscore a structural coherence. He still uses the images that
he has employed all along: the cave, the horse, light and dark
contrasts, the sea, the monster, and other elements taken from
nature and the court. And perhaps what is most striking about
the myth and novelesque plays are their visual effects.

Many of the visual elements, if considered, carefully, are
only a vivification of the imagery. Lindabridis' flying castle
is a marvelous image of the palace in which Segismundo found
himself in La vida es sueño. What is El Fauno in El castillo de
Lindabridis but a visual rendering of the wild side of man
formerly represented by dressing a character, like the above
mentioned Segismundo, in skins? Faetón's flight across the sky
in Apollo's chariot is a dazzling representation of a verbal
image alluded to many times in earlier plays.

Yet in these works there is definitely something more than a
simple transference of verbal imagery into ingeniously designed
sets and props. Since the audience not only hears about nature,
the gods, and the universe but also sees these things and people
presented in plastic form on stage, they sense that all of nature
is intimately involved in the outcome of these plays. In the
myth dramas this is especially so because the gods and semigods
that appear in the works have their correspondence in the natural
processes. In El hijo del sol Faetón, the audience takes a

journey along with the impetuous young man to the throne of the Sun God. In the settings where the events occur, the audience takes for granted the dazzling palaces, beautiful thrones, and supernatural beings:

> Descúbrese el teatro del Cielo, con la luna y algunas
> estrellas, y salen por lo alto, en dos elevaciones,
> Climene y Eridano, y en medio, en la parte superior,
> la ninfa Iris (1895b)

> Córrese en el foro la mutación del palacio del Sol;
> y en un trono, a quien guarnecen las imágenes de los
> signos, se descubre Apolo, y canta la Música (1896a)

In Eco y Narciso the audience is not surprised when Narciso turns into a flower nor when Eco flies off the stage to take on her role that gives her her name. In these plays, the brilliance of the stage design and the marvelous things that happen to some of the characters are an organic part of the natural whole of the world of the play.

A close examination of the imagery in these works will also disprove the idea that the plays somehow represent either a rococo decadence[50] or a failure of the playwright's imagination[51]. For not only does all of the beauty and variety of Nature and the cosmos enter through the visual imagery, but also some of the most striking and beautiful passages in the works involve the same elements in the verbal imagery:

> el mar, que para engañar
> se finge a veces dormido,
> sus verdinegros damascos
> encrespados y movidos
> del blanco céfiro eran
> espejos de nieve y vidrio...

una transmontada nube,
tan pequeña que al principio
una garza parecía
extendió en trémulos visos
las alas de tal manera,
que los cielos cristalinos
dejó oscuros...   (2108a--Hado y divisa de Leonido y
Marfisa)

There are moments in these last works where the imagery
seems more like that of the early plays than like that concise
and concentrated imagery characteristic of the middle plays.
Some speeches are filled with iterations of images on a theme.
In Judas Macabeo we may remember the four images Jonatas used to
describe the elephant that crushes the life out of his brother:

bárbara losa le oprime,
rústica tumba le acoge,
bruta pira le fatiga
y urna funesta le esconde (7a)

In the later plays, we can find passages where images accumulate
but in these final works, the images describe the beauty or
ominousness of nature which, in turn, is one of the central
motifs and backgrounds against which all things are played and
measured:

Viendo, pues, en una parte
cuánto los hombres repudian
la enseñanza, y viendo en otra
cuánto los dioses la ilustran,
a su alto conocimiento
elevé la mente; en cuya
especulación hallé

las monarquías difusas
del cielo y la tierra, dando
de Júpiter a la augusta
majestad del cielo, el mar
a Neptuno, sus espumas
a Venus, luego la tierra
a Saturno, sus fecundas
mieses a Ceres, sus flores
a Aura, a Pomona sus frutos... (2069b, La estatua de
Prometeo)

The natural order and harmony built into the conception of the world is presented in this listing of gods and their attributes.

Stylized elements and careful balance are two of the hallmarks of the late plays. Balance, in part a control over dualities, is surely a defining feature of Calderón's last works. In Homo Ludens, Johan Huizinga's important work on the philosophy of history, we find that the "savage, the child, and the poet" intuitively understand the "agonistic structure of the universe" in which "the processes in life and the cosmos are seen as the eternal conflict of opposites."[52] Conflict and confrontation, according to Frank Warnke, is "surely the defining feature of the Baroque age, an age which, in spite of its utilitarian, didactic, and polemic concerns, lived in constant awareness of the specific qualities of art."[53]

Dámaso Alonso in his essay on Calderónian drama also recognized that agon or duality is a fundamental characteristic of life, of theater, and of Calderón's comedias in particular:

toda la vida es emparejamiento, y en correspondencia,
el teatro es dual y todo teatro tiende a serlo...
Todo el fundamento del teatro calderoniano, como del
teatro español, es rigurosamente dual.[54]

But the duality we find in the early plays is essentially a
structural one wherein characters appear to fall into two groups
(see El pintor de su deshonra), or where the conflict is between
two men over a woman, galán y contragalán with dama y
contradama to use Dámaso Alonso's terms (see the capa y espada
plays), or where the images also take two categories (light
versus dark in El médico de su honra). In the last plays, the
duality is still alive in imagery, contrastive motifs, structure,
and staging but, there is a crossover effect in that characters
are not always what they first appear to be and images that seem
to imply something good can also imply something evil. In La
estatua de Prometeo, dark images tend to stand for ignorance and
chaos while light and fire images signal wisdom and order. In
the dark cave, however, Prometheus made his statue and from fire
come confusion and war. Prometeo and Epimeteo are twins yet
opposite just as are Minerva and Pallas, their divine
counterparts (2074a). The "monster" in La estatua de Prometeo
is Minerva, goddess of knowledge, in disguise and the "divine
messenger" is really Discordia also disguised (2072a). If we
attend to the images and to their sharing of effects, we are
forced to consider such questions as can good come from evil?
can evil do good? can a god be confused? From the dichotomy
presented by dualities in the early and middle plays, Calderón
has moved more and more into ambiguity, but ambiguity based on
apparent duality.[55]

Drama intends to convey its action, meaning, structure, and
characterization by modes at least one step removed from factual
reality. The very artifice of the stage with the actions,
costumes, and words of actors show this immediately. And though
drama may proceed from historical fact, from legend, and from
myth, it is concerned with the significance and connotation of
experience realized vividly through real people acting and
speaking in "artificial" ways. The dramatist exploits, through
imagery, stagecraft, set design, and costume, the instinct to

visualize, to pictorialize by fusing everyday reality with controlled imagination and artistic logic.

A dramatist of the category of Calderón is restless for new ways of communication with his audience. Though verbal imagery never outgrows its usefulness to Calderón, he turns increasingly to these more complex and visual means of expression in his later plays. Not only do stage design and visual effects become more important in the last works, but also the use of symbolic action achieves new heights. The visual and verbal symbol pictorializes and particularizes an abstract symbol. The symbol "according to strict definition, is an animate or inanimate object; it is a palpable thing and, poetically, 'stands for' something which, though usually no less a part of human experience, is not palpable. What the symbol stands for is a moral, intellectual, or sensuous quality"[56]

Philip Wheelwright says that "Past literature...including myths in protoliterary disguise, offers the advantage of greater definiteness /over the symbolic use of historical events/; it furnishes, to a degree, textual evidence of what certain symbols formerly meant and can again partially mean. Symbols having a literary background and a consequent potentiality of allusive reference may be described as having ancestral vitality"[57]. As Calderón turns toward ancient myth, "past literature," as Wheelwright terms it, the symbolic nature of the last plays is forefronted. Calderón looks even more deeply into man's soul, into his past as presented in myth for the reasons behind love, jealousy, honor, and thus for the sources of man's emotions and drives. Wheelwright adds that symbols may have five main grades of comprehensiveness or breadth appeal and we will see all levels of symbology in Calderón's last works:

> A symbol may complete its work as the presiding image
> of a particular poem; it may be repeated and developed by
> a certain poet as having special importance and
> significance for him personally; it may develop

literary life ("ancestral vitality") by being passed
from poet to poet, being mingled and stirred to new life
in fresh poetic contexts; it may have significance for
an entire cultural group or an entire body of religious
believers; and finally it may be archetypal, in the sense
of tending to have a fairly similar significance for
all or a large portion of mankind, independently of
borrowings and historical influences. (98-99)

In Calderón's case one may think of the dream image in La vida
es sueño as an example of the first type; of the cave image for
the second; of the falling horse image for the third; of honor
images for the fourth; and of blood, light-darkness, fire, water,
or the circle for the fifth. In the last plays, Calderón uses
all of the above-mentioned kinds of imagery and it is the
archetypal image that tends to predominate particularly in the
myth plays.

In these plays, the persons actions, and sometimes the
creatures or gods shown on stage become symbols when they typify
something beyond themselves, as in Prometeo's reading of his and
his brother's birth:

de un parto nacimos yo
y Epimeto, sin duda
para ejemplar de que puede
haber estrella que influya
en un punto tan distantes
afectos (2068a)

The defeat of El Fauno at the end of El castillo de Lindabridis
is a means by which a felicitous outcome may be precipitated but
it is also symbolic of man's defeat of the wild beast within his
breast so that civilization, harmony and order may reign. The
symbol, then, is not something apart from an image or a metaphor,

but rather an extension and intensification of them. The symbol has two meanings simultaneously: it represents what it literally is in the action and it transcends the momentary context to suggest more universal meanings.

Symbols are very suggestive, consequently we must avoid the trap of seeing these last works as simple allegories. Allegory is, essentially, "an outwardly simple story that presents a meaningful theme or a moral notion." Figures in allegory are normally "activated abstractions whose function it is to demonstrate certain traits of character, in which case they are flat, simplified projections, not flesh-and-blood human beings." [58] The aim of allegory is to teach a lesson through stories and pictures. But none of the major characters in the final plays, however, is ever so one dimensional that their reduction to allegorical symbols does not take away too many other powerfully expressed traits and attitudes as to make such a simplification impossible.

Allegory supposes a one-to-one relationship between actions and characters and moral qualities or conceptions. The literal must lead to the nonliteral and the nonliteral cannot be evaluated without reference to the literal. If, as W.G. Chapman has suggested, Narciso is simply vainglory[59], what is the allegorical meaning of his innocence? of his love-hate relationship with his mother? of his rightful desire for freedom? If the moral lesson we derive from El monstruo de los jardines is that "el hado solo se vence al triunfar de sí mismo", what is the lesson derived from the fact that by accepting his role in society and in history Aquiles only confirms and does not deny his predicted fate? Allegorical readings of these plays do more to destroy their depth, their variety, and their multiple meanings than the resulting aphorisms do to edify us morally.

Finally in the last plays, one discovers many references to time. Time also is dual because not only is it the present moment, but it also is cyclical and in that sense eternal. As

we watch the people in the final works, we see two kinds of
characters: those who know how to use time and those that do
not. The prudent man knows not only how but when to act. He is
aware that a decision made at the wrong time, even though morally
correct, can be deadly. And he knows that the failure to act at
all may well be catastrophic too. To decide well, to act
properly on the moment is to use time wisely. In its cyclical
aspect, time is tied to the changes in man from birth to growth,
maturity, reproduction, decay, and death; therefore, time is
linked to the cycles of nature. Since in many of these last
plays the gods of nature take an active role, time, nature, the
gods, and fortune are closely linked.

Man, in many of the last works, must find his role not only
in society but also in the macrocosmic universe. He must face
life directly, as was shown earlier in La vida es sueño.
Freedom in time is conditioned upon a belief in an ordered,
purposeful universe. Life may well be a dream, but it is a dream
with meaning. In that dream we must act prudently and we must
not attempt to avoid the future nor the present, for down that
path of avoidance lies meaningless death.

The fact that many of Calderón's plays as well as many
plays by other Golden Age dramatists, end in marriage is not
merely a convenient way of tying up loose ends. Marriage is
rather a promise of renewal and of continuance. In the last
plays, we have marriages in some of the works and apparent death
in others. In some of the myth plays, the characters "die" in
the final scene, but death, for example, the deaths of Eco and
Narciso, is not the final word. Narciso becomes a flower and Eco
an echo. They become, in other words, integral parts of the
natural processes and, therefore, do not die but only appear to
die. By being transformed, they are reborn and will continue to
live, die and be born again throughout time. The promise of
renewal is everywhere in the last plays. As Apollo sings to the
sun:

> No temas, no, descender,
> bellísimo rosicler;
> que si en todo es de sentir
> que nazca para morir,
> tú mueres para nacer (2076a, <u>La</u> <u>estatua</u> <u>de</u> <u>Prometeo</u>)

and he closes the play saying to all:

> ¡Felice quien vio
> el mal convertido en bien
> y el bien en mejor! (2097b)

Order, harmony, meaningful life and death, and temporary suffering resulting in greater permanent glory are constantly reaffirmed. No more hopeful vision of man's condition could be offered.

La hija del aire I, II

The tendency towards stylization seen in the middle plays
grows even stronger in La hija del aire I, II.[60] E.M. Wilson,
writing on El pintor de su deshonra, notes this trend:

> la pieza es más estilizada, menos naturalista que las
> dos donde la venganza es secreta. El modo en que se
> hacen coincidir efectos de escena, pretendidamente
> casuales, disparo de armas, etc... con el diálogo, el
> experto arreglo de las entradas y salidas... en fin
> el paralelismo repetido de dialogo y situación, todo
> esto hace que la comedia parezca artificiosa, teatral,
> y operística...[61]

But, Wilson hastens to add, if realism has been supplanted by a
stylized symbolism, it is at grave risk that one does not seek
out the meaning of the techniques and devices used in such plays.
La hija del aire is at the same time a glance backward to the
middle plays that preceded it and a preview of the myth and
novelesque plays that are to follow. It is precisely the
stylized elements in the presentation of nature, time, and the
gods that must be fully analyzed if this powerful work is to be
comprehended.

The formal style and structure of the work is noticeable at
once . As the play opens, Menón has just returned victorious
from the war and Nino has come to Ascalón to greet him. Menón
has divided his troops into squadrons and they salute the King
"con salva" (715a). Meanwhile, the country folk of Ascalón sing
and play music of love and adoration. All of this takes place
off stage and, in fact, this music divides the scene since the
martial salutes come from one side and the love tributes from the
other. The voices and later the characters remark on this
division:

y a aquellas salvas de Marte
sucedan las del Amor... (715a)

Allí trompetas y cajas,
de Marte bélico horror,
y allí voces e instrumentos,
dulces lisonjas de amor... (715b)

In Act III, stage division occurs in a stichomythic dialogue between Semiramis and Menón while Irene and Nino look on and comment from their respective hiding places on the edge of the stage (741-43). At the end of the scene, Menón and Semiramis exchange positions on stage so that though Menón entered with Nino and Semiramis with Irene, Menón ends up near Irene and Semiramis with Nino. This formal movement underscores events that will come to pass in the play as one character casts his fate with another.

Part II begins with voices and music competing with the trumpets of war (752). And later in Act I, we have the parallel speeches, from opposite points of view, between Friso and Licas:

Lic: El vencedor
        siempre honra al que ha vencido.
        Esto por merced, señora,
        de haberle alcanzado yo,
        te pido humilde.
Friso: Yo no
        que también le rendí ahora,
        sino que su singular
        error castigues, porque
        nadie se atreva en la fe
        que les has de perdonar.
Lic: Vence, dos veces piadosa.
Friso: El castigo es el vencer. (758)

Like the unexpected gunshots in El pintor de su deshonra, Friso receives unexpected answers to his questions. In Act II, he asks, "¿Quién quitó de la cabeza / el laurel a Ninias?" and Flora calls out from above, "Friso." (769a). In a parallel fashion, Friso later wants to know "dónde estoy, quién me llamó / y quién esta mujer fue", to which Semiranis enters saying "Yo, Friso, te lo diré." (772b).

To what end the division of the stage, the contrasts of music, the parallel dialogue, the chance answering of rhetorical questions, the mirror scenes? In the first case, while the music and drums compete off stage, Semiramis breaks out of her prison on stage to comment on the effect of the two kinds of music on her:

> confusamente los dos
> me elevan y me arrebatan:
> éste, que dulce sonó,
> con dulces halagos, hijos
> de su misma suspensión:
> éste, que horrible, con fieros
> impulsos, tras quien me voy,
> sin saber dónde, y que iguales
> me arrancan el corazón
> blandura y fiereza...
> ésta adormece el sentido.
> ésta despierta el valor
> repitiendo los ecos
> del bronce y de la canción. (716a)

Semiramis, imprisoned in the cave since birth, is nascent man showing his two sides: care and compassion versus violence and war. The external stimulus provided by the music and the drums on either side of the stage is internalized by Semiramis and expressed as the basic dichotomy inherent in all mankind, the capability of doing good or evil. Semiramis, here, is at a moral ground-zero; in which direction she will be inclined is the crux of the play.

In the second case, that is, in the stychomithic dialogue, Nino has asked Menón to feign hatred of Semiramis and, in a like manner, Irene has told Semiramis that Menón already has a lover and that she too must "pasar del amor al odio" (741a). Both speakers, Menón and Semiramis, however, are torn since they still care for each other. This internal strife is convincingly shown in the first part of their encounter, all of which is in the form of a "stylized" series of asides:

> Sem: (Ap.)
> ¿Habrá rigor más violento?
> Men: (Id.)
> ¿Trance habrá más riguroso?
> Sem: (Id.)
> ¿Que haya de dar a entender
> yo que ingrata correspondo?
> Men: (Id.)
> ¿Que haya de decir por fuerza
> yo, que lo que estimo enojo? (741b)

As they play out the roles cast upon them, neither Irene nor Nino can believe what they are hearing since neither is privy to the plans of the other and both are surprised that the two speakers express hatred rather than love. They encourage them to carry their expressions even further. Irene tells Semiramis:

> Vuelve a llamar, y asienta
> que no trate en ser tu esposo (742b)

and Nino advises Menón:

Vuélvela a hablar: dila que

no has de hacer el desposorio (742b)

The confusion felt by Semiramis and Menón, and expressed in their dialogue, is reflected in Irene's and Nino's surprise as the two speakers exchange positions on stage at the end of the scene. This lengthy scene shows the inner anguish of all the characters, an anguish caused by love and by ignoble actions of ones' superiors. The dialogue, then, while being a device reminiscent of the love scenes in the early capa y espada plays, points to coming events, to character change, to internal strife that will become externalized, to events being shaped by pressure, and to the powerful effect of passion and of self-centered love.

The music at the beginning of Part II, helps firmly to establish Semiramis' character as the sum of all the lessons she learned in the first part of the play. She is war-like, passion driven, and ambitious. At the same time, the sweet music contrasts a moment of peace and tranquility with the reigning atmosphere of war and chaos that characterizes the second part of the work. And finally, the unexpected answers to Friso's questions focuses the audience's attention on the close relationship between Friso and Semiramis and on the role of fate in the play. In the first example, Friso has just commented on fortune, "Quién no teme a la fortuna / sus iras? (768b), and in the second, he wonders what events and which person could have brought him to such a fearful place. Semiramis enters saying, "Yo."

Though these chance events smack of almost unbelievable coincidence, Calderón has not retreated to a world of casual chance or of convenient tricks. But rather, like in El pintor de su deshonra, he is seeking to show the greater themes and questions of the play. Here, the confusion, chaos, and seeming chance quality of many of the events, shows on a microcosmic

scale a battle raging between the gods in which each is seeking a
victory through their control of the actions shown on stage.

In La hija del aire, there are a number of mirror scenes.
Menón first discovers Semiramis in her labyrinthine abode and
later Nino too enters "lo intrincado del monte" (733a) to find
Semiramis. In Part II, Lidoro is first defeated by Semiramis and
then he conquers her. Semiramis was imprisoned by Tiresias in
Part I and she imprisons herself in Part II. Besides underlining
changes in character as they respond first one way and then
another to similar situations and besides reflecting the rise and
falls in Fortune that a person may suffer, these repeated scenes
also force an awareness of the dual role of time in the plays.

In the present play, time in its dual aspect enters in many
ways. For example, the gods have foretold Semiramis' future:

> Venus te anunció...
> que había de ser horror
> del mundo, y que por mí había
> en cuanto ilumina el sol,
> tragedias, muertes, insultos,
> ira, llanto y confusión...
> Que a un Rey
> glorioso le haría mi amor
> tirano, y que al fin vendría
> a darle la muerte yo (716b-717a)

And this foreknowledge gives Semiramis the opportunity, by the
prudent exercise of free will, to change the outcome:

> pues advertida
> voy de los hados míos,
> sabré vencerlos (725b)

Semiramis leaves her prison at Menón's side apparently grateful to him for her freedom, but immediately afterwards, she wonders if she has only exchanged one prison for another (727a). She leaves her hiding place, for a noble reason, to save Nino.[62] Later, when Semiramis agrees to the postponement of her marriage to Menón, her ambition overcomes her better judgment:

> Si el Rey quiere honrarnos,
> Menón, con mercedes tantos
> no a mi presunción le quites
> la vanidad de lograrlas (737a)

Later she deserts Menón and decides to marry Nino saying to herself:

> (Yo haré, si llego a reinar,
> que el mundo a mi nombre tiemble) (749a)

In Part II, she abandons her rule but not for the noble reason of letting her son, the rightful heir, rule, but because she knows him to be weak and effeminate (760-61). His rule will thus be a punishment upon those who hate her. She later regains her rule by disguising herself as Ninias and then forces her troops into an unnecessary battle.

Semiramis is, then, presented with several moments of decision and in nearly each case, she chooses to act out of passion and not out of reason. 'Ladrona me he de hacer de mi fortuna" (733b) she says, and shows herself to be time's slave, not its master.

For contrast, Lidoro (Arsidas) and Lisías are shown as prudent men who know surely when to act and when to wait quietly for more propitious moments. When Nino gives Ascalón, Lisías' countryside, to Menón, the circumspect Lisías says:

> Aunque el ver he sentido
> que mi patria hoy a ser haya venido
> vasalla del vasallo,
> callaré, pues no puedo remediarlo (738b)

Lidoro, the defeated King of Lidia, feels too the "cólera de la fortuna" (721a). He finds Nino's sister, Irene, hurt and alone, but instead of taking vengeance against her, he saves her life. Subsequently, he falls in love with her, hears her complain about Menón's wandering attentions, but decides to bide his time before declaring his true feelings:

> Mas no
> es tiempo de que me atreva
> ni aun a pensarlo (732a)

And, when he has the chance to join Estorbato to make war on Nino, he again decides that the time is not yet ripe:

> Callaré oculto hasta que
> la ocasión descubra el modo
> que mejor me esté (740b)

Both these men know that only when the time is right can an action be prudently undertaken and that until that moment arrives, they must accept the present adversities. Despite Lidoro's humiliation at Semiramis' hands, he awaits coming events, he trusts in cyclical time, believing in a design beneath the confused surface which fortune shows to man:

> que ninguna
> vez se puso la fortuna
> de parte de la razón (758a)

> que pasar de extremo a extremo
> as de la fortuna oficio (763a)

When the time is right, he acts decisively and carries the day.

Fortune also plays a large part in the play and all of the characters pay due homage to the goddess.[63] The work chronicles the rise and fall of the fortunes of Menón, Nino, Semiramis, and Friso all of whom rise only to fall. Lidoro and Irene, on the other hand, fall and are then elevated by Fortune. In Semiramis' case, she is living in a cave, is rescued by Menón, loves him, must reject his love, is wed to the King, becomes ruler, is deposed, rises to rule again, is defeated and then dies. Her death, symbolically enough, is in part caused by her physical fall from a precipice. Lidoro is defeated by Menón, saves Irene, falls in love with her, yet cannot declare his love, saves Nino (the man responsible for his initial defeat), is freed, is recognized by Semiramis and chained like a dog, is freed by Ninias only to be imprisoned again by Semiramis, escapes, defeats the Queen, and marries Irene. The rises and falls in their fortunes are in tune with the notion of cyclical time already discussed and with the image of the wheel of fortune. Man, through time and fortune, must discover the "uses of adversity" in order to rise above the momentary problems. He can never halt time as Menón foolishly wishes to do:

> y tu diosa Fortuna
> condicional imagen de la luna,
> estáte un punto queda (719a)

Man must see time and fortune for what they are and integrate himself into the cosmic rhythms.

The images of fortune and of time form part of the pattern of the play as do the images of the prison, the labyrinth, the sun, fire, light, and darkness. Semiramis goes from the dark

138

cave to the warmth, love, and light of the day and then back once
again into darkness in the course of the two parts of the play.
Menón moves from glory and light to darkness and blindness.
Once more there is a cyclical aspect to these actions that
reflect nature. It is nature, in fact, that infuses this entire
work. Semiramis, after all, was born into a warring world since
the beasts and birds fought over her at her birth and as a
horrible eclipse blotted out the sun:

> que estaba todo
> ese globo cristalino
> (por un comunero eclipse,
> que al sol desposeerle quiso
> del imperio de los días)
> parcial, turbado, y diviso...
> y a mis gemidos
> acudieron cuantas fieras
> contiene el monte en su asilo,
> y cuantas aves el viento;
> pero con fines distintos,
> porque las fieras quisieron
> despedazarnos y herirnos,
> y las aves defenderlo,
> estorbarlo y resistirlo (724)

Animal imagery forms a strong undercurrent throughout the
play. Semiramis, like Segismundo, first appears dressed in skins
and she is called a monster. And later after she has changed her
bestial dress for a lovely gown, Chato reminds us:

> Pues yo me acuerdo de cuando
> eran pellejos de lobo (739a)

While her outer form may have changed, she is still the same wild person under the silks and jewels.

Many of the descriptions of the atmosphere use animal images to underscore a wild and forbidding aspect. Night is made into a large, black bird which "las alas nocturnas extiende" (746a). Volcanos spew forth fire which seems to be "pájaros de fuego" (750b). Arrows shot into the air become first clouds and then night because of their number, "que las nubes de sus flechas / son noche alada del sol" (II, 757b). Even people are animalized as Lidoro is chained and made to act like a dog (758a). When Semiramis expresses her rage at having to leave the throne, it is with animal images that she best describes her feelings:

> Un basilisco
> tengo en los ojos, un áspid
> en el corazón asido (761a)

There is not in this work a single, unique nature image that is the central image, but rather nature is omnipresent and the more evil aspects or elements outnumber the more positive ones: aves, brutos, caballos, estrellas, fieras, flores, fuego, fuentes, golfos, gusano, hojas, jardines, jazmín, laurel, lucero, luces, luna, mar, monstruo, montañas, montes, naturaleza, nieve, noche, oro, pájaros, garras, picos. pieles, piedra, rayos, ramas, rosa , rubí, sol, trueno, viento.

One major difference between this play and both El mayor monstruo del mundo and La vida es sueño is that, in the earlier plays, both El Tetrarca and Segismundo were, at times, like animals but they were only compared to them. In this play, Semiramis is a direct descendant of the nature gods and, therefore, her relationship with Nature is stronger than that of the other two characters. Nature battles for and with this character in a way not seen before.

As a part of the natural processes, love forms an integral aspect. Love and reproduction point to regenerative time since through the birth of his children, man can continue to exist even though the individual must die. Both pairs, Nino-Semiramis and Lidoro-Irene produce male children, but the offspring of the first pair is effeminate and imprudent, like his parents (ironically, of course, since he is effeminate while his mother is strongly masculine),[64] while the child of the second pair is, like his parents, noble, valiant, and discreet. Nature has reproduced in kind.

In their attitudes toward love, great differences exist among the characters. Lidoro is patient, self-effacing, and constant in his love for Irene while Menón, Nino, and Semiramis are driven by lust. For the latter characters, love is seen in conjunction with destruction, inconstancy, and tyranny. The images they use to describe love characterize them more than they know. The prophecy stated that Semiramis' love would turn a noble king into a tyrant (716b), Menón claims that his imprudent act of not leaving when he is ordered to do so in "traición de amor" (747a). Semiramis herself is, after all, the product of tyrannical lust, "de bastardo / amor de amor mal nacido" (716b), and Nino's love of her is described as violently destructive:

> es un ardiente fuego,
> es un abrasado rayo,
> que sin tocar el cuerpo
> ha convertido en cenizas
> el corazón acá dentro (724a)

The link between love and death is further explored in Part II where Licas says that "amor y muerte / eran los más parecidos" (761b). And finally, love like Fortune's wheel is, for many, inconstant, "que no hay cosa más mudable / que amor" (783b).

That nature and love appear so often in the image pattern of the work is to be expected since Semiramis is an "hija de Venus" (748b) and her mother, Arceta, "fue consagrada a Diana" (724a). Arceta was loved by a young man who worshipped Venus and who prayed to the goddess to give him Arceta. Venus could not do so but she did arrange for him to meet the nymph in a wild and unpopulated area. There, "como tirano" (724a) the young man raped Arceta. From this forced union sprang Semiramis and at her birth, all nature took sides in a battle over her. The beasts fought for Diana who wished to destroy the child, and the birds fought for Venus who successfully defended her life. In the battle we see what Semiramis herself terms a "civil guerra /de/ los dioses" (724b).

The gods are present not only in the description of the battle raged at Semiramis' birth but also in the prophecy, in the imprisonment of Semiramis, and in many of the speeches uttered by the characters. If the gods do control nature, then one may well surmise that when Nino's horse bolted or when the storm arose at the end of Part I, that these events were not chance ones. In fact, in this play, no fewer than eight mythological characters are mentioned: Apollo, Belerophon, Jupiter, Lucina, Mars, Tiresias, Venus, Vulcan.

The presence of so many of the gods can be tied, then, to the previous discussion of time. Since most of these myth figures are linked closely with nature and to the Summer, Fall, Winter, Spring cycle, the concept of continuing, regenerative time is reinforced by their mention. Nature, time and the gods are metaphorically and symbolically linked to the outcome of the conflicts in this work.

At the beginning of this section, reference was made to El pintor de su deshonra and later to La vida es sueño and El mayor monstruo del mundo. La hija del aire, I, II is a look back to the plays of the middle period and a preview of the later myth and novelesque works to follow. The parallels to La vida es sueño are striking, the role of prophecy and of violent nature recalls El mayor monstruo, but there are differences. In the prophecies in the earlier plays, the men who read the stars were easily capable of making mistakes; here, on the other hand, the gods themselves tell the prophecy:

> Venus mandó que estuviera
> oculto, porque Diana
> le amenazó con tragedias (731a)

In the myth plays, the gods do not err. Even though Semiramis knows beforehand, she cannot control her ambition long enough to take effective action. The main character of this play is not a mere mortal, but rather a descendant of the gods. The cave, as Gwynne Edwards says, may represent "man's spiritual prison, the chains of Original Sin and imperfection with which he is born" (57), but Semiramis cannot escape. She cannot translate her free will into positive action.

The roles of the gods, of time, of fortune, and of nature fuse directly into the myth plays as does the growing stylization of the play. There is a shift from the plays of the middle period towards the restorative powers of good, towards the foreknowledge that no matter how bad the momentary actions may seem there is a controlling order and justice and harmony that will right the wrongs. The trespasses against natural law provoke chaos until the final retribution is visited upon the disrupter. In the middle plays, there are yet questions hanging over the future: is Isabel's confinement in a convent at the end of El alcalde de Zalamea truly justified emotionally to the audience? Has Segismundo acted correctly in jailing the rebel soldier? Is it right for Gutierre to marry Leonor? Are social order and honor sufficiently "restored" in El pintor de su deshonra? In La hija del aire, when Semiramis dies, justice on a personal, national, and universal level has been done. Order is restored and Lidoro, a truly good and noble man, will set things right. If there are nagging questions about free will, one can point to the fact that the characters are in a pagan world where non-Christian gods rule absolutely and where man is subject to fate.

The growing stylization helps to create a distance between the world of the audience and the world of the play. One of the advantages of the use of the pagan world and of myth and stylization is to allow Calderón a freedom to go beyond the mimetic representation of the middle plays.

At a key moment in the conflict between Menón and Nino, the former makes a telling statement about the changes afoot in these dramas:

> cansado está
> el mundo de ver en farsas
> la competencia de un Rey,
> de un valido y de una dama.
> Saquemos hoy del antiguo
> estilo aquesta ignorancia,
> y en el empeño primero
> a la luz los efectos salgan.
> El fin de esto siempre ha sido,
> después de enredos, marañas,
> sospechas, amores, celos,
> gustos, glorias, quejas, ansias,
> generosamente noble
> vencerse el que hace el monarca.
> Pues si esto ha de ser después,
> mejor es ahora: no haga
> pasos tantas veces vistos. (736b)

Calderón is changing and, as Gwynne Edwards states, La hija del aire "in scope, in sheer theatrical virtuosity..., in the

grandeur of many of its situations, in the sweep and size of its
characters, and in many passages of magnificent language, it is a
mature realization of those varied dramatic skills which
Calderón acquired during the thirties and can be viewed all the
better against that perspective" (15). The play is a compendium
of the past, to be sure, but it is also an indicator of the
future.[65] Images and their relation to real event, leit motif,
and symbol are stronger than ever in this work. Imagery and
action, imagery and character, imagery and theme, imagery and
structure constantly buttress one another throughout the play.

En la vida todo es verdad y todo mentira

The restorative pattern brought about through time, fortune, and prudence in La hija del aire I, II, is again examined, though with new techniques, in En la vida todo es verdad y todo mentira (1659). As the play opens, the body politic is headed by a cruel and barbaric tyrant bent on a revenge murder. In the end, order and harmony are restored as the rightful heir is brought to power. As in La hija del aire, there is an air of historicity established from the outset but this nod toward mimesis must allow enough flexibility so that the transition from a representational to a symbolic mode can operate. The role of Lisipo as magician is an imaginative break from the play to which this work bears the closest resemblance, La vida es sueño.[66] Special emphasis is drawn, through the magic scenes, to levels of reality, to time, to contrasts. There is, besides, a strongly emblematic quality to the fantasy, the cave, the court, the earthquake, and to the leaky boat cast into the sea, as well as to the horse and the mountains. The division provided by the contrasting characters of Heraclio and Leonido, basically one good and one bad, calls attention also to the artifice. The audience has entered a world in many ways different from that presented in La vida es sueño. Here, the strange and the miraculous can occur and the emblematic, symbolic qualities of some of the characters, actions, and settings is more pronounced. Focas is the tyrannical man-beast; Heraclio, the noble son of a noble man; Leonido, the treacherous son of a treacherous father; Lisipo the failed, ambitious astrologer.

Calderón pairs characters in the play -- Heraclio with Cintia, Leonido with Libia -- though there are several scenes where the established pairs crisscross. Three of these characters are children of people who appeared in the "historical" past that is recounted in the course of the play. Heraclio is Mauricio's lost son; Leonido the lost son of Focas;

and Cintia the child of the former ruler of Trinacria. Focas, with ulterior motives, joined Cintia's father in war against Mauricio and upon winning, he not only took over control of Trinacria, but also went on to conquer Constantinople where Mauricio had ruled. Lisipo, whose daughter is Libia, also had problems with a governor, Federico. When he predicted the downfall of the ruler, he said that the only way to avoid his fate was to swear allegiance to Focas. The interrelationships and the character pairing show that the tyrannized children are drawn together and that the offspring of the man-beast Focas is attracted by the Diana-like child of the astrologer. While the pairing is not quite as black and white as suggested by this summary, there is the suggestion of a basic good versus evil conflict that springs from the past to continue in the future.

Inherent in the past-present, father-child situations is the theme of repeated time. Cintia is terrorized by Focas and must yield to his power as her father in the past was forced to yield. Focas casts Heraclio into the sea and Leonido, following in father's footsteps, also proves himself to be cunning and treacherous. But the children, through fortuitous and prudent use of ocasión, are able to right the past wrongs. Heraclio kills the tyrant Focas and marries Cintia; Leonido swears allegiance to Heraclio, and Lisipo is forbidden from practicing "sus ciencias" (1151b) in the new society that arises.

The symbolic character pairing also occasions certain moments in the play that allow us to compare the two males and to try to decide which is Mauricio's and which Focas' son. In Act I, Heraclio is drawn to the war-like music while Leonido is attracted to the softer tones of love songs. On this point, Cruickshank notes that the drums and trumpets attract Heraclio "as befits the son of a line of emperors"[67] and that the sweet music draws Leonido "because the descendant of a tyrannical usurper should prefer a soft and lascivious life" (112).

Yet Calderón does not tip his hand as to who is who, and the audience, like Focas, is kept in the dark about the two young men's parents. Thus, the audience is forced to weigh carefully a character's actions and statements to try to decide the rightful heir. These emblematic, balanced scenes, then, are not affected because audience participation in the artifice of the stage is reinforced. They too want to learn the answer to the mystery. In earlier plays, like La dama duende and La vida es sueño, the public was privy to the answer from the outset and there it watched one character wrestle with questions of conscience. The pairing of characters carries the audience in two directions and makes it closely examine and consider each and every statement.

In the scenes wherein two men are to be compared, they speak in parallel form:

    Her: Pues si tu luz me amedrenta...
    Leon: Pues si tu luz me acobarda...
    Her: ...presto verás que no ha sido
          vil temor el que me ha dado...
    Leon: presto verás que el que ha estado
          suspenso, Lidia atrevido...
    Her: ...que de cuantos te han seguido,
          ninguno ha de llegar. /Vase/
    Leon: ...que ninguno ha de pasar
          el término que pasaste. /Vase/

    Leon: No basta, señor. ¿No tiene
          este palacio ventanas,
          por donde, volando, vuelva
          más presto?
    Her: Leonido, aguarda,
          que viene sobre seguro
          de embajador, y no agravian
          los motivos de su dueño

en su boca. (1136b-37a)[68]

As the action progresses, Leonido's growing drift toward
tyranny and violence and Heraclio's movement toward compassion,
self-governance, and <u>mesura</u> are stressed. The two men become
symbolic of their father's characters and of the man-beast
dichotomy in Focas.

The inner conflict, reflected in the Leonido-Heraclio
duality, is shown in one way or another in all of the characters.
Cintia must publicly pay homage to Focas:

> En hora venga dichosa,
> tanto que halle a su obediencia,
> con siempre rendido afecto,
> su patria a sus plantas/puesta/ (1110a)

at the same time that she chafes under the yoke of the tyrant:

> (¡Oh temor, cuánto me fuerzas,
> viendo el poder de un tirano!) (1110a)

Likewise, Lisipo knows the future but will not reveal what he has
foreseen and Libia is a beautiful woman but also a fierce
huntress or "marimacha de estas selvas" as one of the <u>graciosos</u>
calls her (1117b).

These divisions are also shown in the title of the play and
in many of the statements made by the characters. When Heraclio
and Leonido talk about women, the former says that woman must be
"la caricia y la terneza... /que/ deja / segundo ruido en al
alma" (1115) and the latter declares that women are frightening
and torment the soul. Astolfo admits that they are both right
since women at the same time are: "hermosura-fiera, amigo-
enemigo, vida-muerte, regalo-dolor, paz-guerra, triaca-veneno"
(1116a).

When they enter the dream-palace, Heraclio asks,

> Lo que veo y escucho
> ¿es verdad, o es vanidad
> de mi fantasía? (1133b)

to which the chorus responds, "Verdad." Leonido then queries,

> Los asombros con que lucho,
> ¿son, cuando en tal confusión
> el sentido los admira,
> mentira o verdad?

and the chorus answers, "Mentira." (1133b).

Heraclio learns to distrust his senses and, like Segismundo, to put his faith in the nonphenomenal while Leonido opts for the pomp and ceremony of the illusory world and, thereby, inevitably loses. Heraclio says,

> No hay humano sentido
> que ser mentira o verdad
> pueda afirmar... (1144b)

Besides these two main characters and their speeches, other elements in the play symbolically underline the verdad-mentira duality. Lisipo's prophecy that Federico would lose his battle with Focas is true and false: false in the sense that Federico's troops emerge victorious, and true in that Heraclio, and not Federico, assumes the throne (see Cruickshank, 119). Focas decides correctly that Leonido is his son but for false reasons as Astolfo notes, "Será la primera verdad / que la mentira había dicho" (1146a). The dream-palace is thought to be real while the characters are acting in it but when they are removed from it, they can recognize its fictionality, though they continue to make decisions in the real world based on events in

the dream world.   Focas   in   particular   makes such judgments
knowing full well that   the   palace   was   an   illusion.   In   the
illusion scenes, Heraclio protects Focas, and Leonido attempts to
kill him while later, the truth of these actions is denied as the
characters exchange roles.

Dámaso Alonso, writing on this play, notes,

> En el plano fantasmagórico, como hemos visto, Heraclio
> pertenece a los miembros 1 (amor), y Leonido a los
>   2 (odio), pero en el real, al contrario. (si se pasa
> del plano del ensueño al de la realidad, la verdad es
> mentira, y viceversa.)[69]

In   this   work   too, there   is a move towards the division of
the stage that will become even   more   marked   as   in   the   later
plays.   This   stage   division calls attention to the division of
characters, of actions, of motives,   and   of   conflicts.   Though
here   that division is not always constant, it does point out the
way toward an entire system of dualities that will be examined in
the   discussion   of Eco y Narciso.   In this play, for example, as
the action begins, the stage directions state:

> Dentro, a una parte cajas y trompetas, y a otra,
> instrumentos músicos; y salen por una parte Soldados
> y Focas, y por otra, Damas, y detrás Cintia. (1109a)

The conflict between war and love, between Focas and Cintia,
between Heraclio and Leonido, between past and   present,   present
and   future,   between   appearance   and   reality   is   tentatively
suggested, emblematized, as it were, in the staging as well as in
all   of   the   other   elements that make up this play. The effort
that the dramatist makes at balancing opposites, never giving   an
absolute   color   to one or the other, this stylization shows that
Calderón is moving away from the representational, mimetic plays

toward the symbolic, nonrepresentational, sign-filled works of which the myth plays are the finest examples.

El hijo del sol Faetón

Calderón significantly modified the events of the myth of
Phaeton in his play, El hijo del sol Faetón (1661). It is true
that Phaeton is still a figure of pride, but he is also of an
heroic and sympathetic nature. Simply put, the audience feels
sorry for him at the end of the work or, as Valbuena Briones has
it:

> Su castigo produce más comiseración que satisfacción
> de ver una justicia cumplida (1861a)

This being so, it becomes a thorny task indeed to interpret this
myth play like so many others by Calderón, along strictly
allegorical lines. If, as in the Ovide Moralisé, we see
Phaeton's actions as the rebellion of Lucifer against God (A.
Valbuena Briones, 1861a), we are hard pressed to explain our
sympathies. If we see the myth in Senecan terms wherein Phaeton
is the man who faces up to his fate with strength (ibid., 1861a),
we are equally hard put to justify his overweening pride. The
play is rather more complex than these two suggestions make it
out to be and it simply will not fit easily into any preconceived
allegorical molds without severe losses in complexity and power.
      The imagery in this work is also exceedingly complex.
Nature is once again the central figure and the audience sees
many of her varied aspects in the work. Amaltea is one of the
"dulces dríades" (1863a) and thus of the earth; Galatea, one of
the "bellas náyades" and of the rivers; Tetis, a daughter of
Neptune and of the sea; Phaeton, son of Apollo, god of the sun;
Climene, Phaeton's mother, the animal-woman of the mountains;
Eridano, a priest of Diana and namesake of the river Eridano;
and Iris, "ninfa del aire" (1891a). Since these gods, semi-gods,
and children of gods are emblematized by natural signs, the links
between character and nature could hardly be stronger.

Besides all of that, there is something about the play that
suggests a cosmic rhythm which is seen most vividly in the image
filled passages describing the rising and setting sun:

>   Tetis: Tus honras recibiera,
>
>   si de volver al mar hora no fuera;
>
>   que ya declina el sol... (1871b)
>
>   Clim: Son el primer crepúsculo del día.
>
>   Ya de sus luces bellas
>
>   se van oscureciendo las estrellas,
>
>   en cuya muchedumbre
>
>   una lumbre se apaga de otra lumbre... (1895b)

This same rising and falling rhythm can be observed in the
fortunes of the two men, Epafo (or Peleo) and Eridano (or
Faetón).

In the omnipresence of nature and in the complexity of the
images and symbols, we can observe a considerable change even
from the complexities of, for example, El pintor de su deshonra.
There, the sea was a negative force as was fire. Music and art
images divided the characters more or less into two groups. In
the present play, no such division is completely workable, though
on the surface it may seem that Epafo is closely tied to earth
images and Phaeton to water images. Of the great wealth of
nature imagery,[70] we shall examine six major strands: the
flowers, the river (or fresh water), the sun, the sea, the wind,
and the horse. We shall begin with the most straightforward and
move to the most subtle and complex.

In Act I, Admeto's horse bolts and runs headlong carrying
the King to sure doom:

>   su caballo
>   rompiendo al freno la ley.

de sí arroja... (1867a)

but Admeto is saved by Phaeton though Epafo receives the credit.
In Act III, Phaeton asks Apollo for permission to drive the
chariot of the sun across the heavens. Apollo warns him that the
horses if not completely reined will break from their path and
wreak havoc on the earth (1897a). From the chariot, Phaeton sees
Admeto carry Tetis away and he decides to go to her rescue
thereby losing control of the horses:

> Los caballos
> desbocados y furiosos,
> viéndose abatir el suelo,
> soberbios extrañan otro
> nuevo camino,... (1901b)

The horses, like the passions, need a steadying hand to prevent
them from carrying one violently off to doom.

Admeto is a proud and hard-headed man (even after
discovering that the "monstruo" of the mountains is human, he
vows to keep his promise to sacrifice her to Diana). Likewise,
Phaeton is driven by pride to attempt to take the chariot aloft.
There, he is then consumed by an all powerful jealousy when he
sees Tetis in Epafo's arms:

> Mas ¿qué mucho, si a mis ojos
> a Tetis, ¡ay infelice!
> llego a ver en brazos de otro?
> Y así perdido lo más,
> ni rienda que airado arrojo,
> ni curso que ciego pierdo,
> podrán hacer que sea estorbo
> de no despeñarme al mar:
> y pues ardo yo, arda todo. (1902a)

The caballo desbocado, like other occurrences of the image in earlier plays, suggests pride and its subsequent fall, uncontrolled passion, and a potentially violent end.

In Act II, Phaeton upbraids Tetis and she responds to his words calling him an "Ignorado hijo del viento." She then takes that image and makes of it one of swelling pride, ("que solo a tanta soberbia / el pudiera dar las alas") (1879b). But this image and this one-to-one link between pride and viento is brought into question if a similar occurrence of the image in Act III is carefully examined. There, Galatea calls on Iris, "ninfa del aire" (1891a) to descend from the heavens to aid Phaeton in reaching Apollo's throne. Iris responds in words that recall the original viento-alas image:

> Pues haz que de los vapores
> que tus cristales levantan.
> y meteoros del aire
> en tupidas nubes cuajan,
> uno a la media región,
> donde yo llego, los traiga.
> hasta que de aquesta nube
> los puedan valer las alas (1891b)

Is this positive or negative? Is it connected to pride? One could answer either way. The heavens have sent Iris to help Phaeton and he surely deserves to be recognized by his divine father. On the other hand, heaven's help and his subsequent recognition will lead inevitably to his downfall and to the near destruction of the earth. The words viento, vapores, aire, alas suggest pride but they also suggest the help he deserves to achieve his due place in society.

In a similar fashion, the sea has dual meanings. When Phaeton is burning with jealousy, he wants to "despeñarme al mar"

(1902a), thus the sea is associated with love by being the opposite of the fire of passion and it is connected to death. This link with death is strengthened when Anfión decides to throw his daughter, Erífile, and her newborn son into the sea (1875b). The sea, however, casts them up on the shores of Tesalia where the mother dies but the baby is saved and raised by Eridano (1874b). The sea, as it were, takes pity on the child.

The sea is refuge and home for Tetis as, for example, when news of the monster is brought and Epafo advises her:

> Ya que las blandas delicias
> de tierra trocar se ven
> en escándalos, pasando
> a ser pesar el placer,
> vuélvete, señora, al mar (1866a)

From this quote there might seem to be a land-sea dichotomy but once again, things are not so simple. The sea and land stand in a mutual relationship rather than in an antagonistic relationship in many parts of the play. When Epafo and Phaeton, surrounded by Amaltea, Galatea, and their choruses, see Tetis approaching the shore, they describe her chariot as "aquel escollo" (1863a) or "aquel / peñasco, que su marina / carroza otras veces fue" (1863a). The choruses of the water nymphs, the wood nymphs, and the ocean spirits join in a mutual harmony: "Sea uniendo a sus dos coros / la armonía de los tres" (1865b). And both Galatea and Amaltea pay homage to Tetis. This is significant since the first two represent the rivers and the flowers of the Earth. It seems that a hierarchical system is being invoked. Admeto later adds to the general feeling about the superior position of the sea when he queries, "¿cuándo el mar no es árbitro del día?"

The variety and complexity, observed in the sea imagery, is also to be discovered in the sun imagery. In many passages, the

warming, life-giving, glorious aspects of the sun and of the sun-
god Apollo are stressed:

> Aliento de los frutos y los flores...
> Anhelito suave...
> del bruto, de la fiera, el pez y el ave (1896b)

> Marinas ninfas de Tetis,
> saludad al Sol hermoso... (1899b)

The sun is the light that takes away the darkness from the earth:

> dueño de la luz del día,
> la sombra y la noche rompo (1900b-1901a)

And, all of the mymphs of the earth, sea, and rivers pay due
homage to the sun (1899b).

Imagery linking Phaeton and Apollo to the sun is to be
expected but the sun also serves as an image for others in the
play. Galatea and her river nymphs, for example, are called
"hijas del sol". In a lengthy passage that begins on 1879a and
goes to 1881b, the sun is alternately used as an image for Epafo
and then for Tetis.

But the sun is also fire and as such can destroy:

> la cercanía del solio
> de la ardiente luz de tantos
> desmandados rayos rojos
> montes y mares abrasa... (1901b)

> De cuantas veces el agua
> vengo del fuego el destrozo
> el del agua hoy venga el fuego (1901b-02a)

And once more the dualistic aspects of life and death in one
image are manifest. This paradoxical, balanced imagery is
characteristic of the other images in this play and of most of
the imagery in the plays of the last period.

In this same line, one notes that while the flowers and
plants pay homage to Tetis (1863-64), later they become a trap
for her:

> Ven con gente, que encubierta
> detrás de unas verdes ramas
> (que yo haré crecer la noche
> y florecer la mañana...)
> el paso impida,
> cuando huyendo de ti vaya (1894b)

The flowers are also images of the future and as such both
positive and negative. Phaeton says that both he and Amalte can
learn lessons from the flowers since for him "pueden ser mañana /
pompas las que hoy sombras ves" but that for her, the reverse is
true, "hoy puedes ver sombras / las que eran pompas ayer"
(1867a). When Epafo is declared the rightful heir to the throne,
he returns to the mountains, where everyone celebrates his
ascension. Those who celebrate his return wear flowers in their
hair, "coronados de flores, / rosas, lirios, y azucenas" (1880b),
but do the flowers suggest positive or negative values, pomp or
true greatness?

Similarly, the rivers pay homage to Tetis (1865b); they
favor and aid Phaeton where the flowers and trees helped Epafo;
they are a means of escape for Tetis (1894a); they are part of
Climene's downfall (1884a); but they can be imprisoned by ice
(1876b); and they are all but destroyed by fire (1902a).

Nature is both positive and negative; she both gives life
and takes it away.[71] Once more through nature and her cycles,
through the emphases on night changing to day and vice versa,

through the rises and falls of the characters, the audience
becomes aware of a cosmic rhythm and of a cosmic order and
harmony. As in nature, the momentary pain and suffering
(disorder) is to be countered by a harmonious ending in which
right order is restored.

Can we say that all is well if the play ends in death? The
last scenes of the work do present certain problems, but if we
bear in mind the natural rhythms at work throughout, solutions to
our questions are to be discovered. First, Epafo marries Tetis,
and, significantly enough, that is the very last action in the
play. We suggested, in the introduction to this period, that
marriage implies continuance and renewal. It is vital to note
that in this play we witness a marriage between a noble,
chastened prince and a divine daughter of Neptune. This marriage
(though of a lesser magnitude than would have been one between
Phaeton -- half divine -- and Tetis) offers a harmony in the
union between heaven and earth. After the saddening death of
Phaeton the audience is promised a return to love and order
between man and the gods.

Second, Climene, Galatea, and the náyades are transformed
into trees and, therefore, do not die:

> Y aun convertidas en troncos
> de álamos blancos...
> Serán
> desde hoy sus cortezas ojos
> que las lágrimas destilen
> del ambar (1902b)

This transformation rightfully emphasizes the melancholy of the
scene but it also implies a natural regeneration, rebirth in
nature and in myth, of the characters.

Third, Jupiter heard the prayers of both his mortal and
immortal subjects, of both man and nature, and struck down

Phaeton. Calderón adds a moralizing note to Phaeton's death through the mouth of the _gracioso_:

> los discretos
> sacarán cuán peligroso
> es desvanecerse (1902b)

and thus, through the sad end of Phaeton, there is something to be gained besides the salvation of the earth. He serves as a moral exemplum to all men since, if the _gracioso_ could see this, then it follows that anyone can.

Even in Phaeton's death the natural cycle is reflected. He was found by and named after the river Eridano and it is to the Eridano that he returns:

> en el undoso
> Eridano, que la cuna
> le dio, hoy le da el mauseolo (1902b)

Life and death, beginning and end are part of an eternal, unending circle.

If we now compare the distribution of the imagery in this play with that of the plays of the middle period, we find some striking differences. In the first scene of this play, as in the first scene of _La vida es sueño_, we are nearly overwhelmed by the sheer number of images. But as _La vida es sueño_ progressed, especially in the last scenes, the imagery became less frequent. (We noted the reverse of this procedure in _El médico de su honra_: few images at first, and a great many in the climactic scenes at the end.) In the present play, on the other hand, the imagery is ever-present and bursts forth at several moments in the work to show us scenes of packed, dense imagery (see 1863-65, 1874-75, 1880, 1883-85, 1887-88, 1895-96, 1900 for examples.)

Besides this verbal imagery many of the characters in the
work are living representatives of the natural settings in which
they are found: Galatea, Amaltea, Doris, Climene, Phaeton, Tetis,
Apolo, Iris. And, furthermore, there are scenes of powerful
visual imagery as indicated by the stage directions:

> Abrese el escollo y se ve Tetis sentada en una concha, y
> Doris sobre un pescado, y entre las ondas algunas Ninfas
> y Sirenas... (1864a)

> Baja un arco al modo de Iris, y en el medio un globo
> hecho de nubes... (1891b)

> Suben en dos pirámides los dos hasta la nube... (1891b)

> Descúbrese el teatro de Cielo, con la Luna y algunas
> Estrellas... (1895b)

> Descúbrese el teatro de fuego que será chozas y árboles
> abrasados (1901b)

The visual representation of the same images used verbally in the
spoken passages can have only the most striking effect on the
audience.[72] The spectator sees[73] as well as hears about the world
of nature and the world of the gods.

There is a strongly sensual quality to this imagery. All of
the beauty and all of the horror of nature pervades this play
from the monster, the fire, the labyrinthine mountains to the
flowers, rivers, seas, and to such delicate touches as:

> cogiendo vamos
> de las doradas arenas,
> nácares y caracoles,
> corales, conchas y perlas (1877a)

or:

> Aves, pues, llora el Aurora
> decidle al Sol que madrugue,
> porque con sólo cendales de oro
> es justo que llanto de perlas se enjugue (1897b)

We perceive nature from its lowest aspects (1889a) to the god-like view that Phaeton offers us as he guides the chariot of the sun across the skies (1900a).

Man and nature join at the end of the play and the tone is not tragic but rather one of a transcendant melancholy fraught with the promise of renewal and life. Physical death is not the final word.

Eco y Narciso

Dámaso Alonso, in his essay on Calderónian drama, recognized that agon or duality is a fundamental characteristic of life, of theater, and of Calderón's comedias in particular (see p. 154). In Eco y Narciso (1661), the general concept of agon or dualities operates not only in the development of plot and character, as Dámaso Alonso suggests, but it is also manifest in all dramatically important elements in the play. One of the most subtle uses of duality involves the control of audience reaction through the manipulation if irony, aesthetic distance, and the sympathy-judgment response of the public. But, to appreciate more fully the larger, refined dualities of the play, one must first examine the more overt uses of doubling in the work.

Double plots and double love triangles predominate in the comedia, and Eco y Narciso is no exception to this general rule. Everett Hesse says that the main plot of the play treats the love theme with Eco, Narciso, and Liríope as the principals, while the secondary plot is a love-jealousy intrigue featuring Eco, Febo, and Silvio.[75] In the first plot, Hesse casts Liríope in the role of antagonist to the growing love between the two young people. Liríope, however, is not as one dimensional as the scheme suggests since besides being the "terrible mother," she is also the loving, protective mother attempting, futilely, to save her only son from a predicted death.

The secondary plot is also complicated because while Febo and Silvio are competing with each other for Eco's favors, more importantly, they are both exceedingly jealous of Narciso. And, though the two shepherds have some small degree of individuality, they are nearly interchangeable. In one scene, for example, Febo stops Silvio from killing Narciso, and, a few lines further on, the roles are reversed as Silvio protects Narciso from the murderous desires of Febo. Besides, after Eco has listened to the two "hacer finezas," she says,

En ti ni en ti he estimado
consuelo ni compasión
 y puesto que iguales son
del que estima y del que llora
los afectos, hasta ahora
no es de ninguno el listón (1923)

Therefore, while there are indeed two triangles in the play, one can modify the original conception of this basic duality to say that in the first triangle, Líríope is one character with two roles, while in the second, Febo and Silvio are two characters with one role. This modification allows the inclusion of the principal protagonists, Eco and Narciso, in each level of action and highlights the strong sense of unity that Calderón has established in both of the plots and in the structure of the play.

Most critics who have written on this play have noted another level of duality in the contrastive motifs that have been worked into the fabric of the play: amar-aborrecer, ver-oír, hablar-callar, ignorar-saber, agua-fuego.[76] This basic list can easily be expanded to show just how pervasive the pattern is: querer-despreciar, sombra-luz, celos-amor, veneno-medicina, ofensa-lisonja, albricias-pésames, primavera-invierno, monstruo-mujer. The contrasting motifs and the contrasting pairs of words are repeatedly used to prefigure or to summarize actions.

On a wider scale, the entire action of the play alternates between two contrasting settings, the mountains and the valley. Each setting is generally associated with a particular theme: the mountains are linked with fate and the valley with love and jealousy. For example, the first scene of the play takes place in the Arcadian valley where Febo and Silvio set both the theme and the tone:

Febo: Yo también a ella /la cabaña7 vengo
      y de verte a ti en ella celos tengo;

que ya mi _amor_ está desengañado
de que vives de Eco _enamorado_.
Silvio: ¡Oh qué temprano, cielos,
antes que con mi _amor_, di con mis _celos_! (1907,
italics mine)

In the next scene, set in the mountains, Liríope tells
Narciso not to listen to the singing voices that he has heard,
"Porque _los_ _hados_ han puesto / mi mayor peligro en ellas"
(1908). After Liríope is captured by Anteo, she cries out to
Narciso, "¡Narciso, adiós, que me ausentan / de ti mis _hados_",
to which he replies, "¿Pues, cómo, madre, me dejas /.../ sin que
yo dónde estás sepa, / que _los_ _hados_ te han dispuesto / a hacer
de mi amor ausencia?" (1910).

At times even the stage is split. In Act I, Silvio enters
from one side of the stage and Febo from the other. At first
their comments are parallel, but later one sees the love conflict
that divides them (1906-7). In Act III, Narciso is drawn to the
spring and his reflection on the one hand, and to Eco and her
beauty on the other. The stage directions point out the dual
action, "Vuelve a mirar a Eco, y deja la fuente" (1923).

In addition, the props have an inherent duality. In the
third act, both Eco and Narciso go to the spring. For Narciso,
it is a means of quenching his thirst, but when he sees his
reflection in the pool, it becomes the instrument of his fate.
For Eco, the spring is a calm spot to which she retires when
troubled, "A llorar vengo a esta fuente, / en cuya apacible
estancia / suelen mis melancolías / divertirse" (1932). But
when she goes to the spring, she finds Narciso, whom she has been
trying to avoid since he rejected her. Narciso has also gone to
the mountains to escape Eco, for his mother told him that Eco
will cause his death. It is significant, furthermore, that they
meet in the mountains, the setting associated with fate, and that
both characters come to the spring to seek relief: his, relief
from a physical thirst, and hers, relief from a spiritual

anxiety.   Ironically,   the   spring which seems to promise
deliverance from physical or spiritual suffering actually
precipitates the fatal outcome, underscoring, thereby, its basic
duality.

The Arcadian world of the valley is also imbued with a dual
nature. On the one hand, as several critics have pointed out, it
is clearly pleasant and idealistic, and may thus be associated
with the love theme.[77]   As Febo and Silvio tell us in their
opening statements:

> Silvio: Alto monte de Arcadia, que eminente
> al cielo empinas la elevada frente,
> cuya grande eminencia tanto sube,
> que empieza monte y se remata nube,
> siendo de tu copete y tus huellas
> la alfombra rosas y el dosel estrellas...
> Febo: Bella selva de Arcadia, que florecida
> siempre estás de matices guarnecida,
> sin que a tu pompa, a todas horas verde,
> el diciembre ni el julio se le acuerde,
> siendo el mayo corona de tu esfera,
> y tu edad todo el año primavera...(1906)

But the shepherds who inhabit the valley live in fear, for
just at the valley's limits, near Jupiter's temple, exists "el
horrible monstruo fiero / que en él se esconde" (1908). The
area around the temple is called "confusa maleza, ásperas
montañas" with "ásperas entrañas." The beautiful valley is
surrounded by a wild and forbidding forest.

Within the valley, forces are at work that quickly bring
about a complete disintegration of this supposed pastoral
paradise. The shepherds are themselves jealous, competitive,
melancholy, and belligerent. There are, then, powers both inside
and outside the Arcadian valley which threaten its destruction.

Constantly mentioned in the descriptions of this Arcadia is its timeless quality, "a todas horas verde," "todo el año primavera," "este siempre apacible floresta.' But time is yet another element marked by its dual nature in that the valley's timelessness stands in marked contrast to the birthday references that abound in the play. Most explanations offered for the birthday references rely on the fact that the work was presented in celebration of the Infanta Margarita's birthday.[78] While historically interesting, these explanations place the references quite outside the realm of the play in both significance and function (though they do reinforce the interplay between the real world and the world of the play). One does not, however, have to step out of the play to see the functions of the birthday references. Both Febo and Silvio underscore the equivocal nature of the birthday from the first scene. Silvio praises Eco's beauty and calls emphatically for general happiness:

> A pediros albricias mi alegría
> viene de las aventuras de este día,
> pues Eco, en él, zagala la más bella
> que vio luz de la mayor estrella,
> de humana da floridos desengaños,
> un círculo cumpliendo de sus años... (1906)

> Eco hermosa, en quien cifró
> la sabia naturaleza
> la más singular belleza
> que jamás la Arcadia vio,
> el círculo cumplió
> la aurora en tus luces bellas
> tanto mejores, que en ellas
> unos y otros resplandores... (1907)

Febo, however, in a precisely parallel speech, declares that the birthday is an image of the destructive passage of time toward old age and death:

> Pésames viene a daros mi tristeza
> de que la rara y singular belleza
> de Eco, desengañada de que ha sido
> inmortal, hoy un círculo ha cumplido
> de sus años: que aunque de dichas llenos,
> cada año más es una gracia menos. (1906)

> Tu florida primavera
> el invierno ignore frío,
> ardiente ignore el estío,
> porque dure lisonjera
> en su verdor, de manera
> que de la muerte las huellas
> no truequen sus rosas bellas
> sino sus albores... (1907)

This day also has significance because it is the anniversary of the disappearance of Liríope, and Sileno casts a pall over the celebration under way with his sad recollections of his daughter's loss. But on this very day, Liríope is far from happy -- first, because she must admit to her dishonor at the hands of Céfiro, "La vergüenza aquí / me embaraza mucha parte / del contento que hay en mí" (1915), and, second, because she has been separated from her son, Narciso.

Even before her capture, Liríope felt that this was an evil day since she feels compelled to tell her son of the predictions about his fate, "Llegó el día que temí" (1909). And on this day, Narciso is separated from his mother for the first time. He realizes that the day has two opposite aspects: he is able to leave the confines of the cave in the mountains and thereby escape the domination of his mother; however, he must enter the free but dangerous world of the valley to exercise his free will.

In short, this day -- Eco's birthday, the day on which Liríope is reunited with the shepherds and with her father, Narciso's liberation day -- offers a basic duality that can be expressed in terms of joy and sadness, of the celebration of life and the recognition of death, a duality that underlies the entire work.

Besides the birthday references, there are other speeches that point toward the destructive passage of time and away from the peaceful, eternal time of Arcadia. In the middle of the second act, Febo stresses the time theme while he emphasizes his own situation:

> Apenas el invierno helado y cano
> este monte de nieves encanece,
> cuando la primavera la florece,
> y el que helado se vio, se mira ufano.
> Pasa la primavera, y el verano
> los rigores del sol sufre y padece,
> llega el fertil otoño, y enriquece
> el monte de verdor, de fruta el llano.
> Todo vive sujeto a la mudanza.
> De un día a otro día los engaños
> cumplen un año, y éstas al otro alcanza.
> Con esperanza sufre desengaños
> un monte, que a faltarle la esperanza,
> ya se rindiera al peso de los años. (1920)

The changing seasons and the rapidly changing face of nature accent the quick passage of time, the mutability of life, and the lover's condition. The repetition of key words such as cano, encanece, cumplen un año, peso de los años, tie his thoughts about nature to his perception of advancing age and are reminiscent of his earlier speech to Eco (1906-7). He links the seasons to human reactions through the use of <u>mudanza</u> and <u>desengaño</u>. Both the mountain and the lover must have the possibility of "spring" or hope in order to survive successfully the "winter" or disenchantment or rejection. His central proposition that "todo vive sujeto a la mudanza" can be seen as one of the keys to the play: characters exchange safety for danger, happiness for sadness, perfection for destruction, but in so doing they manifest their freedom of choice and of action.

On the other hand, it would appear from Febo's remarks that love could save everyone, and, indeed, love is one of the principal themes of the play. Febo, Silvio, and Anteo express their love for Eco in the first scene, and between Eco and Narciso there springs an instantaneous love. Both Sileno and Narciso love Liríope and she, in turn, loves both her father and her son. But when one examines the way in which the characters express their love, the seeds of destruction once more appear. Febo and Silvio couch their love poetry in the language of competition and jealousy, "celos tengo; / ya que mi amor está desengañado / de que vives de Eco enamorado" and "antes que con mi amor, / di con mis celos" (1907). Sileno's expressions of love for his daughter are tinged with thoughts of sadness and death (1907, 1915), while Narciso's love for his mother is a mixture of admiration, frustration, and fear (1909, 1911).

In contrast, the true love between Eco and Narciso is both immediate and deep, but even it is expressed in the conventional terms of suffering and happiness, of death as well as life:

>   Narciso: ¿Qué será que al verla yo
>   pierdo todos mis sentidos,
>   y este pesar que me hace
>   se le agradezco y estimo...?
>   Eco: Desde el instante que vi
>   la hermosura de Narciso,

vivo juzgando que muero,
muero juzgando que vivo. (1922)

Before the actual fact of the tragedy becomes apparent, the characters, in their diction, have already hinted at their eventual destruction. The love between Eco and Narciso is frustrated at every turn by the actions of Liríope, Febo, and Silvio and cannot flourish in the atmosphere of fear and suspicion that characterizes the Arcadian valley. Love cannot overcome fate; the individual struggle is crushed. Eco and Narciso die and Febo, Silvio, Liríope, Sileno, and the other shepherds are left in the ruins to mourn their passing.

Dualities, then, encompass the smallest and the largest aspects of the theatrical experience of Eco y Narciso. From the simplest repetition of the number two through the standard devices of dual plots and contrasting characters into the physical division of the stage. The existence of these elements could be even further emphasized by focusing on mirror scenes, paradox, or on such linguistic devices as oxymoron, catachresis, and conceit.

Calderón, the dramatist, did understand the "agonistic structure of the universe" and, in his mature years, he fully controlled the elements available to him in the theater. The manipulation of distance, irony, and stage craft as well as the dualities in image, theme, structure, and character provide a rich and complex experience for the audience. Nothing in the play can be named without naming something else that is both its opposite and its equal.[79]

El monstruo de los jardines

   El monstruo de los jardines (1667) is, at first glance, a
strange mixture. It begins with tragic overtones -- a shipwreck
from which only two people escape, an earthquake that signals a
battle between gods over the fate of one man and over the fate of
a nation, a man-beast leaving the confines of his cave for the
first time -- but intermixed with these elements are the story of
a lover's trial, a love of the man-beast for a princess,
beautiful descriptions of nature, songs, and music. In Act II,
the curious mix continues with the struggle of the man-beast to
meet his fate, with prophecies of death both of which alternate
with exquisite descriptions and sea nymph choruses. But most
curiously, from the middle of Act II to near the end of Act III,
it appears as though we have entered the world of the earlier
capa y espada plays with their accompanying disguises, hidden
lovers, bultos in the garden, jealousy inspired sword play, and
comical errors. The play ends, then, with a deus ex machina
appearance of Tetis and with a marriage accompanied by the
promise of death for the bridegroom.
   This strange combination of palace intrigue, prophecy, and
love triangles is played out against the mythic background of
Achilles' role in the Trojan War.   Adding to our wonder are
several references to the "literariness" and therefore to the
inverosimil qualities of the play. Tetis, for example, explains
to Aquiles that she is hesitant to tell him about his background
and the prophecy of his future because, "Temo que / no verosímil
parezca" (1998a) and that his future is a danger to him even
though it appears "en términos de novela" (1998a). Aquiles
responds with "¿Qué importará, si es mi vida / fábula, que lo
parezca?" (1998a).[80]
   As in the other myth plays, the principal images of the work
are taken from Nature and the two primary ones are the cave and
the sea. Lidoro, cast up from the storm hears "tristes gemidos"
issuing from "una cueva, que sellada/ de un peñasco está"

(1989a). The interior of the cave is obviously dark and dank since, when Aquiles emerges from it, he is overwhelmed by the light, color, and variety of nature that surrounds him.[81] The cave has been Aquiles prison, to be sure, but, as in Eco y Narciso, the cave is also representative of safety. Tetis explains that she has kept him there so that he could avoid his predicted fate (1998-99). This conflict between confining safety and dangerous liberty expressed vividly by the dark-light imagery is inherent in the cave image since La vida es sueño.

Here, since the cave is near the sea it thus becomes a synonym for the sea. The gruta overlooks the sea as we can infer from Aquiles' speech on 1992a and the connection cave-sea is a natural one. As the cave is a double-edged image, so too is the sea, on the negative side, death, and on the positive, life. The storm at sea with which the play begins is described in horrific terms of rebellion and war:

> Al lobreguecer la noche
> de ayer, algo más violento
> empezó a inquietar las ondas,
> y todo ese vago imperio
> a amotinarse, no sólo
> contra mí, mas contra el cielo,
> pues en odio de sus luces,
> gigante de agua soberbio,
> se roza con las estrellas,
> montes sobre montes puestos (1987b)

The sea, according to Lidoro, wished to put out the light of the stars, wished to rebel against the very gods themselves. The sea takes the lives of the other crew members of Lidoro's ship and, we will remember, Astrea, Deidamia's cousin, also perished at sea (1999a).[82]

But from the death of the young maiden comes Tetis' plan to disguise Aquiles that he might be near his beloved Deidamia. From the depths of the sea, she calls forth a chorus of sea-nymphs and they together fashion a beautiful ship and gather clothes and riches with which to adorn Aquiles:

> Que con los más suntuosos
> adornos, joyas y telas
> que en los archivos del mar
> la hidrópica sed encierra
> a aqueste bruto diamante
> pulir tratéis... (2000a)

And Ulises cannot help but focus on the beauty of the sea scene he observes from afar:

> Tropa de marinas ninfas
> es la que hacia la ribera,
> alegremente festiva,
> llevando el monstruo se acerca.
> Tras ellas iré...Aunque en vano
> será, pues en hombros de ellas
> ya al mar se introduce, donde
> hermoso bajel le espera... (2000b)

> Ya engolfado en alta mar,
> tan favorable navega,
> que siendo delfín que nada,
> parece neblí que vuela... (2001a)

As the sea had before cast up the unfortunate Lidoro and as it had cost others their lives, now it lovingly escorts Aquiles to Deidamia's side. The sea delivers up its treasures with which he is to adorn himself and it is bountiful and beautiful. There are, in total, thirty occurrences of "mar" and seven of "mares" all in Acts I and II. There, they create atmosphere, clarify certain aspects of characterization, and underscore the relationship of the individual to nature.

The sea, on the one hand rebellious and war-like, and on the other beautiful and rich, can be linked to the general background against which the play is set: the Trojan War. Constant references to war are found throughout the play, but Ulises makes them come alive in a way analogous to the visual presentation of the cave in the first two acts. In those acts, the earth opens, "abre una roca Aquiles, y sale a la boca" (1991a). As the cave and its occupant are emblematized by this action, the war too has its visual symbols, the sword and the shield. Both are used by Ulises to test Aquiles but, more impressively, they and the test scene are introduced by drums and horns. Ulises, at this moment, is determined to flush out the hidden Aquiles and he decides to do so in an ingenious way:

> Con esta imaginación
> han trazado mis astucias
> dos instrumentos: el uno
> de curadas pieles rudas,
> y el otro de retorcidos
> metales... (2006a)

He has the drums and horns sounded and everyone stops in amazement. The drums are beaten three more times and Aquiles finally shows his true nature as he also explains the symbolic meaning of the accompanying sounds:

> aqueste es el idioma de la guerra
> que a grandes voces llama,
> pues su concreto grave,
> mezclando lo horroso y lo suave,

>el pecho anima, el corazón inflama,
>
>y a muerte apellida
>
>en glorioso desprecio de la vida (2017b).

As with the visualization of images mentioned above, the drums, like sound effects used in other words from this and from earlier periods (see El pintor de su deshonra, for example), bring about the vivification of the idea they symbolize -- war, honor, sacrifice -- and a change in the character that hears them. Once again the visualization of imagery and its presentation in other non-verbal forms expressively concretizes one of the play's main concerns.

The songs in the play also bring the central themes into sharper focus. The first song is about Venus and Marte (1986a) and shortly thereafter we are made aware of the battle raging between these two gods (1989b-90a , a possible tie to the Trojar War might also be made). Cintia and Sirene sing so that Deidamia might rest, but their song points to concerns about love, sadness, and deceit:

>Desdichado
>
>del que no vive engañado...
>
>¿Qué importa si oyendo estoy,
>
>Nise, tu agrado amoroso
>
>que tú no me hagas dichoso,
>
>si yo pienso que lo soy? (1991a/b)

The nymphs in Act II sing of the transformation of Aquiles into the "monstruo de los jardines" from the "monstruo de las selvas" (2000a). So these last two songs have dealt with deceit, love, transformation, and sadness, major themes in all of the play. The song Aquiles overhears in the garden is effectively glossed by him and by Deidamia whom he has gone there to meet. This serves to underscore their concerns at that moment. And, even the song to Hymen and the subsequent one about love and jealousy focus our attention on the characters' problems at that juncture in the action.

Part of the function of the stage machinery, of the instruments, and of the songs is to give the illusion of expanding the stage itself. There is a sense of amazement in the characters that see and hear these things, to be sure, but the amazement is not restricted to the characters since the audience also experiences a sense of wonder. We hear instruments play off stage and we "see" things that happen off stage through the descriptions given us by those on stage. In Act I, for example, we hear the effects of the storm at sea before we ever see a character appear on stage. We also hear five or six different voices before Lidoro appears. We hear Aquiles voice coming from the cave before we see him, just as we hear songs about Venus and Marte before seeing the chorus. Much of the action of the play takes place off stage and the sounds, descriptions, and songs just like the painted scenery and mechanical devices broaden the stage to encompass all the world about it.

Since many of the actions take place off stage, we find 38 occasions of "Dentro" as a stage direction. This corresponds to 13 uses of "dentro" in La vida es sueño, to 1 in La desdicha de la voz, and to 19 in La hija del aire I. We can observe that in the later plays there are, in general, many more occurrences of dentro than in the earlier ones, 38, for example, in El hijo del sol Faetón. As the actions of the plays expand to encompass the offstage world and, by implication, the surrounding world of the audience, they are drawn into the work more and more. They listen with rapt attention to Ulises' description of the sea nymph chorus carrying Aquiles off to the sea. The audience listens because it seems that the action is taking place just out of their field of vision and that if they had Ulises' vantage point, they too could see what is happening. The descriptions of things not seen on stage are not new in Calderón's theater -- we may remember the description of Enrique's fall in El médico de su honra -- but in works that are so strongly visual, so strongly theatrical as this one, these events seem even more "real."

The noticed repetition of images and techniques in earlier works and repeated, though at times modified, in the late plays should caution us against the idea of "development" as a steady, upward movement towards perfection. Rather we should think in terms of the way these dramatic devices obey differing prerequisites of expression, characterization, structure, and atmosphere of the particular drama under study. We cannot explain differences between A secreto agravio secreta venganza and El monstruo de los jardines by simplistic notions of technical advancement; we must see, in contrast, that images and technical devices demonstrate different modes of conception of the particular dramas.

In the present play, to cite one brief example, Calderón uses the standard techniques of the capa y espada plays to achieve his ends. When Aquiles enters the world of the court, when he changes from the monstruo de las selvas to the monstruo de los jardines, his character and the entire atmosphere shifts to conform with the refined world of the palace. There, disguise, bultos, sword play, love songs, love triangles, are the norm as the characters are in the Madrid of the earlier cape and sword plays. Underscoring this shift are the riddles posed during the latter part of the play. Aquiles tells Deidamia that she need only look around her to discover the identity of her true lover. But Deidamia sees only Astrea (Aquiles in disguise). Aquiles then says:

> Pues si tú dices que estamos
> solas, y yo que está aquí
> tu amante, bien fácil es
> la enigma de descubrir (2008a)

But Deidamia, like Manuel in La dama duende, cannot so easily decipher the riddle. Adding to her confusion at that moment is Lidoro's unexpected entrance (similar to other unexpected entrances in earlier comedies).

The riddle, however, is more central and more important to the conflict than it was in La dama duende. For here, the fate of a nation depends on the discovery of Aquiles' identity and upon his deciding to face up to his role in the war. Therefore, the riddle, the "proverbios" as Ulises calls the chance answers to his rhetorical questions, underlie the whole concept of the play and do not detract from its movement or meaning.

Calderón once more uses a particularized diction to help characterize his creations. Lidoro, for example, is a man totally dependent upon outward appearance. He adopts his disguise only for reasons of "Parecer." For him, the exterior appearances are the interior truths:

> que fuera necio
> quien a vista de su dama
> y más al lance primero,
> llegare con el desaire
> de llegar pobre...

>   Encubrir
> mi nombre, hasta que escribiendo
> a mi padre, sus asistencia
> me adorne de lucimientos
> dignos de decir quien soy (1989b)

Another aspect of Lidoro's character is that he speaks in aphorisms:

> ¡Oh qué cierto
> es donde todos mandan

```
nadie obedece! (1988a)

            pues callar
con celos no lo hizo nadie (2013b)

Pero no me quejo, no,
de la fortuna, aunque veo
ejecutadas en mí
sus sañas; de mí me quejo;
que es merecido castigo
de quien imprudente y necio,
sin mandar al viento, fía
sus esperanzas al viento (1987b)
```

His knowledge is reducible to shallow truisms and to appearances; his self-concept is egocentric and self-pitying; his actions are imprudent and fruitless. His diction gives him away immediately.

For contrast, we can look at Aquiles. Though at the beginning, due to his long imprisonment in the cave, he seems a little simple and ingenuous (see his reaction to the sleeping Deidamia and the fainting Sirene), he impresses us with his sweeping descriptions of nature. Where Lidoro found nature to be unpolished and rude (1986a), Aquiles sees the beautiful light of the sun, the blue shimmer of the sky, and the enormous loveliness and variety of nature (1992a). Aquiles is also a quick study and rapidly outgrows his initial simplicity. He accepts disguise immediately for through it, he can be near the woman he loves. And, in fact, the disguise seems to convey to him all of the cleverness and quick-wittedness commonly attributed to women, as he himself recognizes:

```
(presto (¡Oh fácil ser!)
hábito de hablar me dio
el hábito de mujer.) (2007b)
```

He responds quickly to stressful situations and he poses sly
riddles before he finally reveals himself to Deidamia.

Aquiles cannot remain long disguised since his true nature
is constantly forcing itself to the surface. He is torn between
his love for Deidamia, which he believes he will have to give up,
and his growing desire to take his rightful place in history.
His vocabulary takes a turn to war-like phrases in the last part
of Act III. Notice the images in his response to Ulises:

> Los sucesos
> que improvisadamente asaltan
> el muro del pensamiento
> la mayor ruina que dejan,
> después de saquearle el pecho,
> es no dejarle palabras...
> el valor no lo consiente,
> representándome...
> la guerra que me apellida
> la grande fama que pierdo.
> la patria que desamparo... (2019b)

These later speeches contrast with the earlier ones wherein his
constant wonder with the world outside of the cave deals mainly
with nature, with the people with whom he comes into contact, and
with questions about his imprisonment. Once more, diction and
imagery as they change from Act I to Act II, demonstrate
character growth and awareness.

The return to old modes, like the capa y espada techniques,
and their new usage within the framework of the later plays shows
that Calderón uses techniques for different ends and for greater
organic unity in different periods of his development. The use
of myth once again illustrates his control over distance and
finally, the stage craft too contributes to the new world where

these actions take place. The theatrical effects are used both for the visualization of images and for the expansion of the stage world. The audience finds itself in the unique position of being both inside and outside the created world.

Hado y divisa de Leonido y Marfisa

Hado y divisa de Leonido y Marfisa (1680), the last play
that Calderón wrote, is a visual extravaganza. If the
interpolated commentaries that Hartzenbusch found with the
manuscript are by Calderón, as he says that they are, then it is
obvious that he was as enchanted and excited by the visual
effects of the play as was the audience. After describing the
white and gold arches studded with what appear to be precious
stones of the gabinete real in Act II, he says

> No puede la retórica hallar, entre la variedad de sus
> tropos, frases que imiten la menor parte del lucimiento
> que allí hubo... (2115a)

Hyperbole, perhaps, but this sentence is proof of what was said
earlier about Calderón's changing attitude toward stage craft
and its function as an organic, necessary part of the dramas of
the last period.

The visual effects throughout reiterate the action and
development of the play. In Act I, one sees a forest, "frondoso
y oscuro, y a trechos claro, imitando la naturaleza" (2098a).
Trumpets, drums, and voices are heard, and Leonido appears in
full armor on horseback. The beast he is riding seems in danger
of falling and indeed, the fall shortly occurs. Thus, one of the
principal symbols used in many of the plays where it is only
described is employed yet again here, but with the exception that
it is presented live, on stage:

> se vio despeñar con tan proprio precipicio, que se
> volvió en lástima la admiración, cayendo arrojado del
> caballo, y él, libre del peso que le oprimía, solicitó
> buscar la libertad por las intrincadas breñas (2099a)

All of the symbolism -- fall from fortune, danger, out-of-control passions -- is still present, but the presentation is even more vivid.

The entire first act is filled with visual images of danger in nature: the peñascos, the sea, the gruta, the interior of the cave, and finally that combination of myth and Nature, Megara mounted on the serpent. In classical mythology, Megara was one of the three Furies who sprang from the drops of blood shed when Cronus mutilated his father. They were the avengers of crimes, especially of murder and of crimes committed against a blood relative.

Argante summons Megara not to avenge a crime, but rather to prevent one, to stop Leonido from giving over Marfisa to Mitilene. The family tie from the ancient myth is still preserved -- Marfisa and Leonido are brother and sister -- but Megara is more the savior than the furious avenger. She obeys Argante, about whom more will be said later, and she has the powers of nature at her call. Megara conjures up "lluvias, rayos, relámpagos y truenos", all images of chaos, or in her words of "la lid de los elementos" (2113a).

In Act II, the scenery begins to shift from scenes in nature, to harsh nature, to the palace. When Leonido returns to Marfisa's cave, for example, he finds himself in the woods on the mountain (2114a), but when he forces open the mouth of the cave, instead of "lo funesto de la cueva" as in Act I, he discovers a sumptuous palace about which the exclamation on the first page of this section was written. Here, all of the images associated with the courtly life:"arcos, frisos, colores, luces, esmeraldas, rubíes, amatistas, turquesas," richly dressed ladies, music, choruses are to be found. Besides the transformation of rude nature to polished rooms, one is again made aware that outward appearances are truly deceiving. Beneath the crude exterior lies all of the intricate beauty of the palace room. In a like fashion, beneath Marfisa's rough clothing and behind Leonido's

unknown birth lie true nobility of spirit and royal blood.
Imagery is paradagmatic in this instance.

In the last act there are two brief returns to the forest
but most of the action takes place in the palace. There is not,
however, an absolute separation of the court from nature. In Act
I, courtiers, princes, and princesses act out their roles in the
midst of a natural surrounding; in the second act, there is the
palace room in the cave; and in the final act, the courtly
architecture of the real palace is decorated with Nature's
finery. A garden appears:

> donde parece que envió la Naturaleza todos sus primores...
> Había abajo balaustres que guarnecían las entrecalles,
> y encima balcones volados llenos de macetas de flores...
> Toda la fábrica del jardín era de arquitectura,
> columnas revestidas de flores, hechos los arcos del propio adorno
> tejiendo entre ellos naranjos y cipreses, de suerte
> que no se embarazaba la arquitectura con el follaje (2131b)

Once more the stage reflects the characters and their
changes. As the polished natural adornments cover the courtly
architecture, so too Argante who before was described as a wild
man, "monstruo, / de brutas pieles cubierto" (2151b) is now
dressed "de gala" (2149a). Similarly, Marfisa who was also
dressed in skins enters wearing the courtly armor of Leonido.
Both the finery of Argante and the armor borne by Marfisa are
symbolic of the court yet they cover supposedly wild people from
hostile nature. As the polished nature that covers the
architecture modifies and beautifies its surroundings, so too
does the dress modify and elevate the two characters. This blend
of nature and the court is the golden mean sought throughout this
play and many others.

As wild nature gives way to its more polished aspect, as the
actions move from the forest to the palace, so too do the

characters change from a state of confusion, isolation, and
"wildness" to one of peace, integration, and civility. Once
more, there is no easy dichotomy of nature versus court of wild-
man versus courtier in this scheme. For, though nature appears
to be harsh and forbidding in the first part of the play, it is
precisely that nature that saves man. As Megara rescues Marfisa
at the end of Act I, so also do Megara and nature prevent
Mitilene's and Arminda's armies from battling each other at the
end of Act II. There, the volcano erupts spewing fire and smoke
creating chaos and fear in the soldiers. All are forced to
retire from the field and the ensuing respite provides entry for
Casimiro in the final act. Nature the apparent destroyer
becomes nature the true protector. And, on the other hand, the
palace, for all its beauty and grace, not only holds the true
princess but also the treacherous Florante and the angry Arminda
both bent on Leonido's destruction.

This intermingling of effects visible in the staging and in
the action is furthered by other structural elements in the work:
the careers of Arminda and Mitilene and their opposite feelings
about Leonido; the lives of Leonido and Marfisa; the cyclical
aspect of time (war, peace, war, peace and the final marriages);
and by the balanced deaths of Arminda's brother and Leonido's
aide and close friend.

As the scenes change from the forest to the palace, so too
do the characters change identities. Leonido, son of Casimiro,
as an infant was carried away by a lioness. He was found and
raised as a knight by the Duke. Later he becomes the poor
"náufrago" to Mitilene and the "soldado alemán" to Arminda. He
is forced to do battle with "himself" finally to emerge as the
rightful heir to the throne. Marfisa, the other lost child of
Casimiro, was spirited away by Argante, the man-beast / magician-
seer. She became his student, the woman-beast of the cave, and
later the "dama" of the cave-palace scene. After donning
Leonido's armor, she becomes Leonido, fights the "soldado

alemán" (Leonido in disguise) and finally is recognized for the true princess that she is. The characters, their roles, and their clothing change as fast as the stage design.

For this brother-sister pair, two visual images are the constants to which they cling in the surrounding chaos: the medallas and the armor. For Leonido, his armor represents his honor and his valor and these are the values that Marfisa sees in them when she puts on the same armor:

> hurtándole las armas
> de Leonido, suplir
> la ausencia (que no acaso
> él me las trajo aquí,
> y ellas a él me trajeron),
> porque nunca decir
> pueda el traidor, que vive
> y que dejó de ir
> de temor (2145b)

The medals are the symbols of their unknown parentage and as they exchange them as tokens of their mutual good faith, they are surprised to see that the one they gave away is exactly like the one they received. The two siblings believe in each other, trust and love one another from the moment of their first encounter and this constancy is reflected by the constancy of the medals.

As Leonido and Marfisa are ignorant of their parentage, so too is Casimiro ignorant of the fate of his lost children. His role is a multifaceted one since at the same time he is bereaved father, father figure to the nation, King, and restorer of peace. He functions much like a deus ex machina figure in the myth plays. Nothing is known about him, for example, until he appears in the final act. He is also uncle to Arminda and Mitilene, an older, prudent man whose presence inspires peace and trust. The song with which he is greeted provides a vivid contrast to the stridency of the war scenes at the end of Act II. It is emblematic of the man and his desires for peace, love, and order in times of strife:

> De los palacios de Venus,
> Casimiro, invicto César,
> a las campañas de Marte
> en hora dichosa venga. (2130a)

He believes in the providential rule of a power greater than himself:

> pues es cierta
> cosa que nada haya acaso
> en quien todo es providencia (2133b)

And yet his return to Trinacria brings back all the painful memories of his earlier loss (of his children). Even though he brings peace to others, he cannot yet find it in himself, but time will cure even his suffering. He feels joy upon greeting the "soldado alemán" though he cannot find reasons for his intense feelings":

> ¿Qué es esto que el corazón
> me está diciendo acá dentro
> en mudas calladas voces?
> Mucho estimo, y nada entiendo. (2140a)

As he offers to judge the battle between the soldier and "Leonido", he once more characterizes his larger role, "seré juez y tan padrino / suyo en la lid como vuestro" (2140b).

As in the myth plays, Casimiro, like the gods, must uphold natural law and yet temper his judgment because he is dealing with members of his own family. And, like the gods, it is he who,

in this instance, makes the future by revoking a prediction
rather than fulfilling it (thereby interrupting the cause and
effect chain so firmly established in the middle period plays).
Argante says that Marfisa must either live by killing or kill and
die, to which Casimiro replies:

> No prosigas, no;
> que pues revoco el decreto (2151b)

If Casimiro has the role of a "god" in the play, then for
sure Argante is the prophet magician figure so familiar in these
last works. Argante stole the infant Marfisa and has kept her
hidden in his cave. To his charge, he is both father and jailer,
as was Liriope to her son, Narciso, in Eco y Narciso. His
speeches are filled with ominous images of the disaster he
foresees: "temí, pavor, red, enemigo, fatal término," and with
images of power and control. It is Argante who can summon Megara
who, in turn, can call on nature to do her bidding. Argante's
references to cyclical time, to magic, to secrets, to conjuring
suggest his role but, like all of Calderón's prophets, he cannot
see exactly how the outcome will occur, nor can he always control
the events about him. He says about Marfisa:

> no pudo toda la ciencia
> de mis mágicos desvelos
> ocultarla (2149a)

and he, like Casimiro, recognizes a controlling power greater
than his own:

> Bien pudiera yo cobrarla /a Marfisa7
> como otra vez hice; pero
> si imperio en Megara tuve,
> en su influjo no me atrevo

> el día que por vencido
> me doy a mayor imperio (2149b)

As a magician, not only can Argante make nature do as he wishes, but also he can conjure up visions of the future. He has Arminda, Florante, Aurelio, and Adolfo appear before Leonido in the cave, but as Leonido seeks to intervene in the vision, Argante reminds him that what he sees is not real, "ni son ellos, / sino aparentes fantasmas" (2121b). But Argante refuses to let Leonido act because, as in other cases, he knows the time is not ripe (2121b). As magician, as "dramatist," Argante cannot give away the end before all of the actions are played out and all of the decisions are made.

His role as "dramatist" underlines the fictional quality of the play. Not only does Leonido see his life as a fiction, "como fábula" as he says, but also the repetition of lines from well-known literary pieces points to this concept:

> Merlín: Tengan lástima de mí,
>   que soy niño y solo
>   y nunca en tal me vi /La niña de Gómez Arias/

> Soldado: ¿Qué me va? La compasión
>   de la sinrazón que han hecho
>   con vos, que en un noble pecho
>   la sinrazón es razón /Feliciano de Silva,
>   Cervantes/

These distancing devices, these allusions to the fictionality of the play plus the vision and the supernatural events underscore the dream-like aspect of the play. But it is not a dream nor is it a fiction for the characters because they endure hardships, sufferings, and anguish before being restored to their positions in society and before peace comes again.

This work, like the myth plays. is not a study in decadence nor in loss of originality nor in rococo, "feminine" degeneration (Valbuena Briones 2096b), but rather it obeys rules other than those used in the middle plays. Here, "as in dreams, queens and kings are our representatives. Their royalty universalizes them. They revive our sense of our own omnipotence, which, though constantly assailed by adult experience, survives in the recesses of personality even after childhood".[83] These plays, their verbal and visual imagery, free us from our "inhibitions and preoccupations by drawing us entirely into /their/ world -- a world which is never fully equivalent to our own although it must remind us of it if we are to understand it at all. It oversteps the limits by which life is normally bounded." (Beer, p.3)

Summary

The purpose of this study has been to demonstrate a developmental process at work in a chronological series of plays by Calderón de la Barca. Imagery and its function have been the central pole around which the discussions turned because imagery lies at the very heart of these poetic dramas. Whether the plays are tragic, comic, or somewhere in between, an image still elaborates on, amplifies, synthesizes, and links concepts and ideas to character, theme, and structure. Through verbal and visual imagery, past literature, social ideas, concepts of the cosmos, philosophies, passions, the personal wants, desires, and quirks of the characters, the setting and atmosphere enter and become part of the fabric of the play.

The idea of development can be justified in the early plays where Calderón was learning to make the more powerful and broad connections between style, meaning, and structure that come to characterize his more mature dramas. The shift from the isolated image, to the "principle of addition," to lists, to patterns as well as the general move from simile to metaphor underscore the evolution toward greater coherence wherein every element echoes in the same or in a different key notes struck by other constituent elements.

Once the artist's skills are internalized, it is difficult if not misleading to continue a "simple" notion of development -- the idea or the implication of development as a stairway toward greater, more celestial unity. In fact, in the middle period it would be fruitless to dispute whether La vida es sueño is more dramatically coherent than El médico de su honra or whether the latter makes more organic use of images than El mayor monstruo del mundo. About the plays of this period it would be more correct to state that each of these works creates its own particular atmosphere and "sound." Different ideas or different facets of drama and theme are stressed in each of those works and thus images and other stylistic devices are ordered in different ways to produce the desired effect. The idea of development as advance is therefore foreign to the mature plays.

It has become obvious, on the other hand, that as time passed and advances were made in stage craft and in stage machinery, Calderón became more cognizant of the effects that could be created through the judicious use of visual apparatus. From the 1650's on, his plays are increasingly more theatrical. It is not that verbal imagery disappears, for, as has been shown, quite the opposite is the fact, but rather that stage craft, sets, and stage machinery add an extra dimension to the imagery and to the plays that simply could not have been done before. Through stage machinery, a cave can be shown being transformed into a garden of delights even as the character comments upon both what he or she sees and on what he or she feels when faced by this miracle. The working together of the verbal and the visual in the last plays is a powerful interaction that alternately draws the audience in and forces them away. The symmetry, balance, and harmony of all the possibilities of the stage culminate in the compelling, glittering dramas of the last period in which myth and romance, man and nature emerge victorious.

Yet a study of imagery or of stylistics is only one step towards a more complete understanding and appreciation of Calderón. This study has been limited to some of the comedias, since I consider the autos to be a subgenre apart, subject to different rules. Neither did this work attempt to place Calderón's developmental process in the framework of other dramatists, nor in the perspective of the development of comedia nor of Spanish theater in general. Such yet to be undertaken studies would yield valuable and fascinating information and might also offer the opportunity to employ the recent critical perspectives of, among others, Barthes, Todorov, Genette, and Harold Bloom.

The dangers of limiting a study to imagery are obvious and thus, while attempting to avoid some of the pitfalls, the present work does not pretend to be exhaustive either of Calderón's imagery or of his style, for a full study of the imagery in most of the plays examined herein would require a book-length analysis of each. I have tried to reach a compromise between the complete study of each play and the brief summary of all the elements in each. If this study has suggested the processes at work in the plays and pointed to other areas of investigation that could be fruitful, it will have accomplished its purpose.

That <u>Hado</u> <u>y</u> <u>divisa</u> <u>de</u> <u>Leonido</u> <u>y</u> <u>Marfisa</u> is different from <u>Judas</u> <u>Macabeo</u> is apparent to even the most casual reader. How Calderón went from his earliest dramas to his final ones has hopefully been partially illuminated here. Calderón's achievement of mastery over his art was a long process but one he undertook with obvious enthusiasm and joy. In the last play he wrote, his love of man, his love of life, and his love of his craft are as apparent as anywhere in his long career. For that, the Spanish stage in particular and world literature in general is infinitely enriched.

FOOTNOTES

[1] Image, Rhetoric, and Drama in Calderón (London: Tamesis, 1977), p. 135.

[2] The Development of Shakespeare's Imagery (New York: Hill and Wang, no date), p. 3.

[3] Theory of Literature (New York: Harcourt, Brace, and World, 1956), p. 188.

[4] In Perspectives on Drama, ed. J.L. Calderwood and H.E. Toliver (New York: Oxford University Press, 1968), pp. 388-405.

[5] On dates for Calderón's plays, see N.D. Shergold and John E. Varey, "Some Early Calderón Dates," Bulletin of Hispanic Studies 38 (1961), pp. 274-86; Shergold and Varey, "Un documento nuevo sobre D. Pedro Calderón de la Barca," Bulletin Hispanique 62 (1960), pp. 432-37; Shergold and Varey, "Some Palace Performances of Seventeenth Century Plays," Bulletin of Hispanic Studies 40 (1963), pp. 212-44; Shergold and Varey, Teatros y comedias en Madrid: 1600-1650, 1651-1665, 1666-1687 (London: Tamesis, 1973, 1974); N.D. Shergold, A History of the Spanish Stage (Oxford: Clarendon Press, 1967); as well as particular editions of individual plays noted in the discussions of those works. The fact is that the date of composition cannot be assigned with absolute accuracy to more than a handful of plays. This study presents a sequence of plays from the early 1620's through 1680 and bases that ordering of works on the above mentioned studies. Among the plays studied, a few comments on dates of particular ones are in order: Judas Macabeo is a possible 1623; El médico de su honra is questionable as to date since there was a performance of a play by the same name in 1629 but this may well be the source play; El pintor de su deshonra was published in 1650 and is probably from the 1646 period but that too is open to question; El monstruo de los jardines was published in 1672 but the exact date of composition is doubtful. (I am indebted to John Varey for his comments in a letter about the dates for these plays.) The dates suggested for the rest of

the plays have been researched by many others and I follow their
suggestions. This study uses chronology as a basis for showing
the developmental process at work but it does not propose to be a
method for dating these or other works. The divisions seen in
Calderón's works are grosso modo as I have indicated and no
absolute frontiers can be posited after or before which Calderón
always uses a particular style. The division of the plays into
early, middle, and late periods is based partly on dates, partly
on style, and partly on convenience. The developmental processes
that I have described, however, will become apparent to the
reader who undertakes a chronological approach to the datable
plays.

[6]All quotes from the plays are from the Angel Valbuena
Briones' editions, Calderón de la Barca: Obras Completas, I, II
(Madrid: Aguilar, 1956, rpt. 1960, 1973) and will be indicated in
parenthesis in the text. References to Professor Valbuena's
introductory remarks will also be so indicated.

[7]See E.M. Wilson and W.J. Entwistle, "Calderón's Príncipe
constante: Two Appreciations," Modern Language Review, 34
(1939), pp. 207-222; Bruce Wardropper, "Christian and Moor in
Calderón's El príncipe constante," Modern Language Review, 53
(1958), pp. 512-520; Elias Rivers, "Fénix's Sonnet in
Calderón's El príncipe constante," Hispanic Review, 37 (1969),
pp. 452-458; and William Whitby, "Calderón's El príncipe
constante: Fénix's Role in the Ransom of Fernando's Body,"
Bulletin of the Comediantes, 8, No. 1 (1956), pp. 1-4.

[8]See the Princeton Encyclopedia of Poetry and Poetics, ed.
Alex Preminger, Frank Warnke, and O.B. Hardison (Princeton:
Princeton University Press, 1965, rpt. 1974), pp. 767-69.

[9]See Clemens, The Development, p. 21-39.

[10]See A. Valbuena Briones, "El tema de la fortuna en La gran
Cenobia," Quaderni Ibero-Americani, 45-46 (1974), pp. 217-223.

[11]See I.A. Richards, The Philosophy of Rhetoric (New York:
Oxford University Press, 1936).

[12]See Philip Wheelwright, The Burning Fountain: A Study in the Language of Symbolism (Bloomington: Indiana University Press, 1954), especially the chapter "Metaphoric Tension," pp. 101-122.

[13]For more see the Princeton Encyclopedia of Poetry and Poetics, p. 490, and especially the bibliography listed on page 494.

[14]Note the exclamations he uses underscoring his constant surprise: ¡Vive el cielo!, ¡Vive Dios!, ¡Cielos!, ¡Válgame el cielo!, ¡Válgame Dios!, ¡Jesús!, and ¡Ay!.

[15]Professor Robert ter Horst in "The Ruling Temper of Calderón's La dama duende," Bulletin of the Comediantes, 27, No. 2 (Fall, 1975), pp. 68-72, states that it is Manuel "whose masculine hierarchy is superior in the art of life and civilization to Angela's chaos." (p. 72). Ter Horst says that Manuel is able to survive through, in part, "his vivid imagination" (p. 70) and his "rational control over human impulse and action" (p. 68). My own view is closer to, though not identical with, Edwin Honig's thoughts expressed in Calderón and the Seizures of Honor (London: Cambridge University Press, 1972), p. 110. Even Manuel's language denies him an "active" or "controlling" role.

[16]For more on this play and on the capa y espada plays, see Barbara J. Mujica, "Tragic Elements in Calderón's La dama duende," Kentucky Romance Quarterly, 16 (1969), pp. 303-326; Bruce Wardropper, "Calderón's Comedy and His Serious View of Life," in Hispanic Studies in Honor of Nicholson B. Adams (Chapel Hill: University of North Carolina Press, 1966), pp. 179-193; and A. Valbuena Briones, "La técnica dramática y el efecto cómico en La dama duende de Calderón," Arbor (1976), pp. 15-26.

[17]See Wardropper, "Calderón's Comedy".

[18]Robert B. Heilman, This Great Stage: Image and Structure in King Lear (Baton Rouge: Louisiana State University Press, 1948), p. 24.

[19]See Peter N. Dunn's Introduction to El alcalde de Zalamea (Oxford: Pergamon Press, 1966), pp. 16-24.

[20]See also A. Valbuena Briones, "La palabra 'sol' en los textos calderonianos"in Perspectiva crítica de los dramas de Calderón, (MaDRID: RIALP, 1965),.

[21]"The Dramatization of Figurative Language in Spanish Theater," Yale French Studies, 47 (1972), p. 196.

[22]See Elenora R. Sabin, "The Identities of the Monster in Calderón's El mayor monstruo del mundo," Hispania, 56 (April, 1973), pp. 269-274.

[23]"Metáfora y símbolo en la interpretación de Calderón", in Actas del primer congreso internacional de hispanistas, ed. Frank Pierce and Cyril A. Jones (Oxford: Dolphin, 1964), p. 145.

[24]See also Everett Hesse, "El arte calderoniano in 'El mayor monstruo los celos'," Clavileño, 38 (Marzo-Abril, 1956), pp. 18-30 and the chapter on this play in his book, Calderón de la Barca (New York: Twayne, 1967), pp. 104-110; Edward H. Friedman, "Dramatic Perspective in Calderón's El mayor monstruo los celos," Bulletin of the Comediantes, 2 (Fall, 1974), pp. 43-49; Raquel Chang Rodríguez and Eleanor Jean Martin, "Tema e imágenes en El mayor monstruo del mundo," Modern Language Notes, (March, 1975), pp. 278-282.

[25]See my article, "Las imágenes en El mayor monstruo del mundo de Calderón de la Barca," Hispania (Vol. 61, No. 4, 1978), pp. 888-97.

[26]Bruce Wardropper in "Poetry and Drama in Calderón's El médico de su honra," Romanic Review, 49 No. 1 (February, 1958), has stated that this play is, in fact, an extended metaphor, p. 4-5.

[27]Wardropper in "Poetry and Drama" points out how the physical fall prefigures the metaphorical fall and how Calderón, "ensures our poetic belief by establishing his more significant images on a nonmetaphorical precedent" (p. 6). The interpretation of the play offered here is also indebted to A.A. Parker's

"Metáfora y símbolo" and Daniel Rogers' "'Tienen los celos pasos de ladrones': Silence in Calderón's El médico de su honra," Hispanic Review, 33 (1965), pp. 273-289.

[28]See A. Valbuena Briones, "La palabra sol and Wardropper, "Poetry and Drama," pp. 9-10.

[29]A.A. Parker in "Metáfora y símbolo" states that Mencía uses "salud" first of all the characters in a metaphorical sense, "En salud me he de curar." I agree with him but would add that this metaphor has been carefully prepared for since the beginning lines of the play. The word appears seven times in Act I and Mencía uses it, though not metaphorically, three of those times. The central metaphors in the play are, to repeat Wardropper, first grounded in nonmetaphorical use.

[30]Wardropper, "Poetry and Drama...", p. 7.

[31]See also C.A. Soons, "The Convergence of Doctrine and Symbol in El médico de su honra," Romanische Forschungen, 72 (1960), pp. 370-380.

[32]"On La vida es sueño" in Critical Essays on the Theater of Calderón (New York: New York University Press, 1965), pp. 63-89.

[33]In Hispania, 49, No. 3 (September, 1966), pp. 421-429.

[34]"The Monster, the Sepulchre and the Dark: Related Patterns of Imagery in La vida es sueño," Hispanic Review, 35 (1967), pp. 161-178, reprinted in Pedro Calderón de la Barca: Comedias, Vol. 19, Critical Studies of Calderón's Comedias (London: Gregg, 1973), pp. 133-149.

[35]See also M.A. Buchanan, "Culteranismo in Calderón's La vida es sueño" in Homenaje ofrecido a Menéndez Pidal, I (Madrid: Hernando, 1925), pp. 545-555; A. Valbuena Prat, "El orden del Barroco en La vida es sueño," Escorial, 6 (February, 1942), pp. 167-192; William Whitby, "Rosaura's Role in the Structure of La vida es sueño," Hispanic Review, 23 (1960), pp. 16-27; Everett Hesse, "El motivo del sueño en La vida es sueño," Segismundo, 3 (1967), pp. 55-62; Joaquín Casalduero, "Sentido y forma de La vida es sueño" in his Estudios sobre el teatro español (Madrid:

Gredos, 1962), pp. 161-184; Charles V. Aubrun, "La Langue poétique de Calderón de la Barca notament dans La vida es sueño" in Réalisme et Poesie au théâtre (Paris: Centre National de la Recherche Scientifique, 1960), pp. 61-76.

[36]Shakespeare's Wordplay (London: Methuen, 1965).

[37]Reprinted in Pedro Calderón de la Barca Comedias, Vol. 19, Critical Studies of Calderón's Comedias, ed., J.E. Varey (London: Gregg, 1973), pp. 191-207.

[38]A. Valbuena Briones (p. 914a) notes that in La desdicha de la voz, there are more complications than there are characters and he lists four of the love relationships: Don Juan-Beatriz, Don Juan-Doña Leonor, Don Diego-Doña Beatriz, Don Pedro-Doña Leonor as well as the fraternal relationships between Don Diego and Leonor and Don Pedro and Doña Beatriz.

[39]The term, "dark comedies," is used frequently in Shakespearean criticism, for example, D.A. Traversi, An Approach to Shakespeare, II (New York: Doubleday, 1969).

[40]For more on the concept of comic pointer, see Larry S. Champion, The Evolution of Shakespeare's Comedy (Cambridge: Harvard University Press, 1970), p. 108.

[41]E.M. Wilson in his chapter "Calderón" in A Literary History of Spain: The Golden Age Drama 1492-1700, coauthored with Duncan Moir (London: Benn, 1971), says that this work, "in some ways the most profound of the wife-murder tragedies -- is too complex to summarize" (p. 112).

[42]See Bruce Wardropper, "The Unconscious Mind in Calderón's El pintor de su deshonra," Hispanic Review, 18, No. 4 (1950), pp. 285-301, especially, p. 291.

[43]The seraphim were associated with fire, love, and proximity to God. She, Serafina, is the woman no man can attain, "tú, conseguida, no puedes conseguirme." I would like to thank Bruce Wardropper for this observation made to me in a letter.

[44]C.A. Soons in "El problema de los juicios estéticos en Calderón: El pintor de su deshonra," Romanische Forschungen, 76

(1964), pp. 155-162, says that Roca cannot capture "el alma tras la representación pictórica" (p. 155), but he certainly seems to in the Hercules painting. What Roca cannot paint, as he himself admits, is perfect beauty.

[45]The dance is the rugero and was performed by pairs who came together and separated, formed culebrillas /y/ coros and is similar in movement to the choreographed scene in the garden between the Prince and Porcia. There. he approached or retired according to the verses she sang. For more on the rugero, see A. Castro y Rossi, Discurso acerca de las costumbres públicas y privadas (Madrid: n.p., 1881) quoted by M. Ruiz Lagos in his edition of the present play (Madrid: Ediciones Alcalá, 1969), p. 154.

[46]M. Ruiz Lagos, in his introduction to El pintor, states that the painting actually appeared on stage (p. 39). P.N. Dunn in "Honor and the Christian Background in Calderón," in Critical Essays, ed. Bruce Wardropper says that Gutierre's killing of Mencía "is a consummation which puts an end to nothing except hope, and it is a new beginning only in a depressing sense. He has to renew, and ask God's blessing on, his alliance with Leonor, which has already yielded honour's bitter fruits" (p. 39). I would agree but would add that no matter how small, there is at least a chance for a future for him.

[47]A.I. Watson, in "El pintor de su deshonra and the Neoaristotelian Theory of Tragedy" in Critical Essays, ed. Bruce Wardropper, says that Don Juan is 'to be allowed to live out the rest of his shortened life without further punishment" (p. 222). What further punishment could there be since life is worse than death for Roca?

[48]See also Frank Casa, "Honor and the Wife-Killers of Calderón," Bulletin of the Comediantes, 29, No. 1 (Spring, 1977), pp. 6-23.

[49]Frank Casa in "Honor and the Wife-Killers" says that "while the lay plays of the Golden Age are infused, as they must be, with the dominant principles of the period, they cannot be made to serve, as do religious plays, theological ends (p. 10). Bruce Wardropper also notes the often unconvincing "critical casuistry" of some interpretations of Calderón's comedias in "Calderón's Comedy" (p. 184).

[50]See A. Valbuena Briones, p.1915.

[51]See James Maraniss's comments in his book On Calderón (Columbia: University of Missouri Press, 1978), p. 87.

[52]English translation (Boston: Beacon Press, 1955), p. 28.

[53]Versions of Baroque (New Haven: Yale University Press, 1972), p. 91.

[54]"La correlación en la estructura del teatro calderoniano,"in Seis calas en la expresión literaria española (Madrid: Gredos, 1970), p. 125.

[55]Freud notes that a shifting from one image to its contrary, an oscillatory movement is a characteristic of dream-thinking, "it may be said to be almost the rule that one train of thought is followed by its contrary." For more on the correspondences between dream-thinking and the creative imagination, see Edward A. Armstrong, Shakespeare's Imagination (Lincoln: University of Nebraska Press, 1963), especially pp. 108-119.

[56]See Edward A. Bloom, et al, The Order of Poetry (New York: Odyssey, 1961), pp. 33-34.

[57]Metaphor and Reality, (Bloomington: Indiana University Press, 1962), p. 98. See also, William Y. Tindall, The Literary Symbol (Bloomington: Indiana University Press, 1955).

[58]Bloom, The Order of Poetry, p. 62.

[59]W.G. Chapman, "Las comedias mitológicas de Calderón," Revista de Literatura, 9 (1954), p. 55.

[60]This play is probably from the same period as El pintor de su deshonra. The inclusion of La hija del aire I, II in the

third part of this "division" of Calderón's works, then, is not based purely and solely on chronology but also on the stylistic tendencies it demonstrates.

[61]"Hacia una interpretación de El pintor de su deshonra," Abaco, 3 (1970), p. 51.

[62]See Gwynne Edwards's introduction to La hija del aire (London: Tamesis, 1970), p. 3. To this study I am most indebted for some of the observations included here.

[63]"Fortuna" appears 14 times in Part I.

[64]See Edwards, pp. 48-49.

[65]I do not wish to belabor the point but I do not wish to be misunderstood either. There is no abrupt or total break with the past, rather there is a steady change visible in the later works of the middle period. All of the techniques used here and in subsequent plays are but outgrowths of artistic knowledge gained in Calderón's long experience on the stage. A shift of emphasis or of focus, yes, but never a complete turning away from the past.

[66]See D.W. Cruickshank's introduction to his edition of En la vida todo es verdad y todo mentira (London: Tamesis, 1971), especially pp. 129-130.

[67]Cruickshank says that Heraclio, "possesses all of the virtues of Aquinas' ideal prince, except for humility, which he attains as a result of his experience with the dream-palace," p. 110.

[68]Many parallel scenes follow: 1115b/1116a, 1122a/b, 1129/1130, 1134a, 1136b/1137a, 1140b/1141a, 1150a/b, among others.

[69]"La correlación en la estructura del teatro calderoniano", p. 125.

[70]Of the many aspects of nature we can list are the following with their frequency of occurrence: sol (63), fiera (46), monte (36), flores (31), mar (21), cielos (18), cristales (18), cielo (18), tierra (17), fuentes (11), playa (9), montes

(9), oro (8), fuego (8), cumbre (8), alas (8), aurora (8), agua (7), selvas (7), perlas (7), risco (6), caballo (5), cristal (5), estrellas (5), ríos (5), rosas (5), nieve (5). References to myth-nature figures also abound: Tetis (52), Eridano (42), Diana (16), Amaltea (16), ninfas (14), Galatea (14), Apolo (13), Faetón (10), Júpiter (10), Doris (9), Iris (6).

[71]The balancing effect, which will be explored more fully in the section on Eco y Narciso, is suggested here by words that convey joy and life versus sadness and death: amor (28), bella (11), dicha (9) norabuena (9), ventura (8), dichosos (7), favores (7), triunfos (6), hermosura (6), etc... versus mal (20), asombro (11), cruel (11), infeliz (11), duda (9), riesgo (9), horror (7), triste (7), muerte (7).

[72]See A. Valbuena Prat, "La escenografía de una comedia de Calderón," Archivo español de arte y arqueología, 16 (1930), pp. 1-30, and E. Orozco Díaz, El teatro y la teatralidad del Barroco (Barcelona: Editorial Planeta, 1969).

[73]Note that forms of the verb ver: ve, vea, vean, ved are used 162 times in the play.

[74]See also, Versions of Baroque: European Literature in the Seventeenth Century (New Haven: Yale University Press, 1972), p. 74. Most critics who have written on the Baroque state that dualities, or an agonistic relationship of certain elements, are key to understanding the art of this period. While there is general agreement about the existence of dualities, there are many definitions of what those dual elements are. See, for example, Heinrich Wolfflin, Principles of Art History (London: G. Bell and Sons, 1932); Wylie Sypher, Four Stages of Renaissance Style: Transformations in Art and Literature 1400-1700 (New York: Doubleday, 1955); Blake Lee Spahr, "Baroque and Mannerism: Epoch and Style," Colloquia Germania, 1 (1967), pp. 78-100; Lowry Nelson, "Góngora and Milton: Towards a Definition of the Baroque," Comparative Literature, 6 (1954), pp. 54-63; and Marketa Lily Freund, "Baroque Technique, Thought and Feeling in

Certain Representative Comedias of Calderón," unpublished doctoral dissertation, University of Colorado, 1966.

[75]"Estructura e interpretación de una comedia de Calderón," in Boletín de la Biblioteca Menéndez Pelayo, 39 (1963), pp. 57-72, and also see Hesse's "The 'Terrible Mother' Image in Calderón's Eco y Narciso," Romance Notes, 1 (Spring, 1970), pp. 1-4.

[76]See Hesse's "Estructura" and " 'Terrible Mother'," as well as Edmond Cros, "Paganisme et Christianisme dans Eco y Narciso de Calderón," Revue des Langues Romanes, 75 (1962). pp. 39-74.

[77]See the articles by Hesse, Cros, and the introduction to the play by A. Valbuena Briones.

[78]Valbuena Briones, introduction, p. 1905; E. Hesse, "Courtly Allusions in the Plays of Calderón," PMLA, 65 (1950), pp. 543-544; Edmond Cros, "Paganisme." p. 43.

[79]For more on this play including a discussion of psychical distance, see my article, "Dualities in Calderón's Eco y Narciso", Revista Hispánica Moderna (1976-77, No. 3), pp. 109-18.

[80]This conversation is followed by references to the "teatros /que/ la fortuna representa' (1998b) and to the fact that "que el mundo en tu historia vea / la más extraña que el tiempo / repite en plumas y lenguas" (1999b). See also 2000b and 2020a.

[81]We may contrast Aquiles' reaction to this surrounding nature (1992) with Lidoro's thoughts about the same setting. While Aquiles sees beauty in the earth, streams, trees, and sea, Lidoro sees only "esta isla bárbara y desierta /.../ sus troncos... /.../ mal pulidos los veo, / sus plantas sin cultura, sin aseo / sus flores" (1986a).

[82]Tetis' violation also occurs near the sea. See also 1998a/b.

[83]Gillian Beer in The Romance (Methuen: London, 1970), has spoken of the effect of such plays and stories on the audience;

see in particular, chapters 1, 3, and 5. For more on the romance qualities of this and other of Calderón's plays, see my forthcoming articles, "Romance Elements in Calderón's <u>comedias novelescas</u>", to appear in a collection of articles in honor of Everett Hesse to be published by the University of Nebraska Press and "Calderón and Shakespeare" to appear in a collection of articles on Calderón to be published by Texas Tech Press.

Selected Bibliography

Actas del primer congreso internacional de hispanistas. Eds.
Frank Pierce and C.A. Jones. Oxford: Dolphin, 1964.

Alonso, Dámaso.Estudios y ensayos gongorinos. Madrid: Gredos,
1960.

---------- and Carlos Bousoño. Seis calas en la expresión
literaria española. Madrid: Gredos, 1970.

Armstrong, Edward A. Shakespeare's Imagination. Lincoln:
University of Nebraska Press, 1963.

Aubrun, Charles V. La comedia española. Madrid: Taurus, 1968.

----------."La Langue Poetique de Calderón de la Barca notament
dans La vida es sueño." In Realisme et Poesie au Theatre.
Paris: Centre National de la Recherche Scientifique, 1960,
pp. 61-76.

Beer, Gillian. The Romance. London: Metheun, 1970.

Blue, William R., "Dualities in Calderón's Eco y Narciso,"
Revista Hispánica Moderna, 3 (1976-77), pp. 109-118.

----------, "Las imágenes en El mayor monstruo del mundo de
Calderón de la Barca," Hispania, 61, 4 (1978), pp. 888-97.

Bravo Villasante, Carmen. "La realidad de la ficción negada
por el gracioso." Revista de filología española, 28
(1964), pp. 264-68.

Brooks, Cleanth. The Well Wrought Urn. New York: Harcourt,
Brace, and World, 1947.

208

Brown, Stephen J. The World of Imagery. New York: Russell and
    Russell, 1966.

Bryans, John V. Image, Rhetoric, and Drama in Calderón. London:
    Tamesis, 1977.

Buchanan, M.A. "Culteranismo in Calderón's La vida es sueño." In
    Homenaje ofrecido a Menéndez Pidal I. Madrid: Hernando,
    1925, pp. 545-55.

Bullough, Edward. "Psychical Distance as a Factor in Art and as
    Esthetic Principle." In A Modern Book of Esthetics. Ed.
    Melvin Rader. New York: Holt, 1952.

Burke, Kenneth. The Philosophy of Literary Form. Baton Rouge:
    Louisiana State University Press, 1941.

Calderón de la Barca. El alcalde de Zalamea, Ed. Peter N. Dunn.
    Oxford:PergamonPress, 1966.

----------La dama duende. Ed. A. Valbuena Briones. Madrid:
    Cátedra, 1976.

----------. En la vida todo es verdad y todo mentira. Ed. Donald
    W. Cruickshank. London: Tamesis, 1971.

----------. La hija del aire I,II. Ed. Gwynne Edwards. London:
    Tamesis, 1970.

----------. El pintor de su deshonra. Ed. M. Ruiz Lagos.
    Madrid: Alcalá, 1969.

----------. Obras completas I,II. Ed. A. Valbuena Briones.
    Madrid: Aguilar 1956.

Calderón de la Barca Studies 1951-69. Eds. Jack E. Parker and Arthur M. Fox. Toronto: University of Toronto Press, 1971.

Calderón y la crítica. Eds. Manuel Durán and Roberto González Echevarría. Madrid: Gredos, 1976.

Casa, Frank. "Honor and the Wife-Killers of Calderón." Bulletin of the Comediantes, 29 (Spring, 1977), pp. 6-23.

Casalduero, Joaquín. Estudios sobre el teatro español. Madrid: Gredos, 1967.

Champion, Larry S. The Evolution of Shakespeare's Comedy. Cambridge: Harvard University Press, 1970

Chang Rodríguez, Raquel and Eleanor Jean Martin. "Tema e imágenes en El mayor monstruo del mundo." MLN, 90 (March, 1975), pp. 278-82.

Chapman, W.G. "Las comedias mitológicas de Calderón." Revista de Literatura, 9 (1954), pp.35-67.

Clemens, Wolfgang. The Development of Shakespeare's Imagery. New York: Hill and Wang, n.d.

Cope, Jackson. The Theater and the Dream. Baltimore: Johns Hopkins Press 1973.

Cotarelo y Mori, Emilio. Ensayo sobre la vida y las obras de D. Pedro Calderón de la Barca. Madrid: RABM, 1924.

Critical Essays on the Theater of Calderón. Ed. Bruce Wardropper. New York: New York University Press, 1965.

Cros, Edmond. "Paganisme et Christianisme dans Eco y Narciso de Calderón." Revue des Langues Romans, 75 (1962), pp. 39-74.

Debicki, Andrew. Estudios sobre la poesía española contemporánea. Madrid: Gredos, 1968.

----------. La poesía de Jorge Guillén. Madrid: Gredos, 1973.

Doran, Madeleine J. Shakespeare's Dramatic Language. Madison: University of Wisconsin Press, 1976.

Friedman, Edward H. "Dramatic Perspectives in Calderón's El mayor monstruo del mundo." Bulletin of the Comediantes, 2 (Fall, 1974), pp. 43-49.

Freund, Marketa Lily. "Baroque Thought and Feeling in Certain Representative Comedias of Calderón." Unpublished doctoral dissertation. University of Colorado, 1966.

Frye, Northrop. Anatomy of Criticism. Princeton: Princeton University Press 1957.

----------. The Secular Scripture. Cambridge: Harvard University Press, 1976.

Frutos, Eugenio. La filosofía de Calderón en sus autos sacramentales. Zaragoza: CSIC, 1952.

Hatzfeld, Helmut. Estudios sobre el barroco. Madrid: Gredos, 1966.

Heilman, Robert B. This Great Stage: Image and Structure in King Lear. Baton Rouge: Louisiana State University Press, 1948.

Hesse, Everett. "El arte calderoniano en 'El mayor monstruo del mundo.'" Clavileno, 38 (marzo-abril, 1955), pp. 18-30.

----------. "Courtly Allusions in the Plays of Calderón" PMLA, 65 (1950) pp. 531-49

----------. Estructura e interpretación de una comedia de Calderón." Boletín de la Biblioteca de Menéndez Pelayo, 38 (1963), pp. 57-72

----------. "El motivo del sueño en La vida es sueño." Segismundo, 3 (1967), pp. 55-52.

----------. "The 'Terrible Mother' Image in Calderón's Eco y Narciso." Romance Notes, 1 (Spring, 1970), pp. 1-4.

Hispanic Studies in Honor of Nicholson B. Adams. Eds. Frank Pierce and Cyril A. Jones. Oxford: Dolphin, 1964.

Holland, Norman. The Shakespearean Imagination. Bloomington: Indiana University Press, 1964; rpt. 1975.

Honig, Edwin. Calderón and the Seizures of Honor. Cambridge: Harvard University Press, 1972.

Huizinga, Johan. Homo Ludens. Boston: Beacon Press, 1955.

Knight, G. Wilson. The Crown of Life. London: Methuen, 1948.

Langbaum, Robert. The Poetry of Experience. New York: W.W. Norton, 1957.

Langer, Susanne K. "The Dramatic Illusion." In Perspectives on Drama. Eds. J.L. Calderwood and H.E. Tolliver. New York: Oxford Univ. Press.

Litterae Hispanae et Lusitanae. Ed. Hans Flasche. Munchen: n.p., 1968.

Mahood, M.M. Shakespeare's Wordplay. London: Metheun, 1965.

Maraniss, James A. On Calderón. Columbia: University of Missouri Press, 1978.

Maurin, Margaret. "The Monster, The Sepulchre, and the Park: Related Patterns of Imagery in La vida es sueño." Hispanic Review, 35 (1967), pp. 161-78.

Mooney, Paul A. "A Reevaluation of Past and Present Critical Opinion on the Comedias Mitológicas of Pedro Calderón de la Barca." Unpublished Doctoral dissertation, Pennsylvania State University 1973.

Mujica, Barbara J. "Tragic Elements in Calderón's La dama duende." Kentucky Romance Quarterly, 16 (1969), pp. 303-26.

Nelson, Lowry. "Góngora and Milton: Towards a Definition of the Baroque." Comparative Literature, 6 (1954), pp. 54-63.

Ochse, Horst. Studien zur Metaphorik Calderons. Munich: Wilhelm Fink Verlag, 1967.

Order of Poetry, The. Eds. Edward A. Bloom, C. H. Philbrick, E. M. Blistein. New York: Odyssey Press, 1961.

Orozco Díaz, E. El teatro y la teatralidad del Barroco. Barcelona: Planeta, 1969.

Parker, A.A. "Christian Values and Drama: El príncipe constante." In Studia Iberica: Festchrift fur Hans Flasche. Eds. Karl-Hermann Korner and Klaus Ruhl. Bern-Munchen: Francke, 1973, pp. 441-58.

--------. The Allegorical Drama of Calderón. Oxford: Dolphin, 1968.

----------. The Approach to the Spanish Drama of The Golden Age. London: The Hispanic and Luso-Brazilian Councils, 1957.

Pedro Calderón de la Barca, Vol. 19: Critical Studies of Calderón's Comedias. Ed. J.E. Varey, Westwood: Gregg, 1973.

Perspectives on Drama. Eds. J.L. Calderwood and H.E. Tolliver. New York: Oxford Univ. Press, 1968.

Picatoste, Felipe. Calderón ante la ciencia. Madrid: Aguado, 1881.

Princeton Encyclopedia of Poetry and Poetics. Eds. Alex Preminger, Frank Warnke, O. B. Hardison. Princeton: Princeton University Press, 1955.

Richards, I.A. The Philosophy of Rhetoric. New York: Oxford Univ. Press, 1936.

----------. Practical Criticism. New York: Harcourt, Brace, and World. 1929.

Rivers, Elias. "Fenix's Sonnet in Calderón's El príncipe constante." Hispanic Review, 37 (1969), pp. 452-58.

Rogers, Daniel. "'Tienen los celos pasos de ladrones': Silence in Calderón's El médico de su honra." Hispanic Review, 33 (1965), pp. 273-89.

Ruiz Ramón, Francisco. Historia del teatro español I. Madrid: Alianza, 1967.

Sabin, Elenora R. "The Identities of the Monster in Calderón's El mayor monstruo del mundo." Hispania, 56 (April, 1973), pp. 269-74.

Sage, Jack. "The Constant Prince." In Studia Iberica: Festchrift fur Hans Flasche. Eds. Karl Hermann Korner and Klaus Ruhl. Bern-Munchen: Francke, 1973, pp. 561-74.

Seventeenth Century Imagery. Ed. Earl Miner. Berkeley: Univ. of Calif. Press, 1971.

Shergold, N.D. A History of the Spanish Stage. Oxford: Clarendon Press, 1967

----------, J.E. and John E. Varey. "Some Early Calderón Dates." Bulletin of Hispanic Studies, 38 (1961), pp. 274-86.

----------. "Some Palace Performances of Seventeenth Century Plays." Bulletin of Hispanic Studies, 40 (1963), pp. 212-44.

----------. Teatros y comedias en Madrid: 1600-1650, 1651-65, 1666-87 (London: Tamesis, 1973, 1974).

Sloman, Albert E. The Dramatic Craftsmanship of Calderón.
     Oxford: Dolphin, 1958.

Soons, C.A. "El problema de los juicios estéticos en
     Calderón: El pintor de su deshonra." Romanische
     Forschungen, 76 (1964), pp 155-61.

----------. "The Convergence of Doctrine and Symbol in El
     médico de su honra." Romanische Forschungen, 72 (1960),
     pp. 370-80.

Spahr, Blake Lee. "Baroque and Mannerism: Epoch and Style."
     Colloquia Germania, 1 (1967), pp. 78-100.

Spurgeon, Carolyn. Shakespeare's Imagery and What It Tells Us.
     Cambridge: Cambridge Univ. Press, 1971.

Studies in Spanish Literature of the Golden Age Presented to
     Edward M. Wilson. Ed. R.O. Jones. London: Tamesis,
     1973.

Sypher, Wylie. Four Stages of Renaissance Style:
     Transformations in Art and Literature 1400-1700. New York:
     Doubleday, 1955.

ter Horst, Robert. "The Ruling Temper of Calderón's La dama
     duende." Bulletin of The Comediantes, V. 27, No 2 (Fall,
     1975), pp. 68-72.

Tindall, William Y. The Literary Symbol. Bloomington: Indiana
     Univ. Press, 1955.

Traversi, D. A. An Approach to Shakespeare. New York: Doubleday,
     1970

Tuve, Rosemond. _Allegorical_ _Imagery_. Princeton: Princeton Univ. Press, 1977.

Valbuena Briones, A. "La técnica dramática y el efecto cómico en _La_ _dama_ _duende_ de Calderón." _Arbor_ (1976), pp. 15-26.

----------. _Perspectiva crítica_ _de Calderón_. Madrid: RIALP, 1965.

----------. "El tema de la fortuna en _La_ _gran_ _Cenobia_." _Quaderni_ _Ibero-Americani_, 45-46 (1974), pp. 217-23.

Valbuena Prat, A. "La escenografía de una comedia de Calderón." _Archivo_ _español_ _de_ _arte_ _y_ _arqueología_, 16 (1930), pp. 1-30.

----------. "El orden del Barroco en _La_ _vida_ _es_ _sueño_." _Escorial_, 6 (February, 1942), pp. 167-92.

Wardropper, Bruce. "Calderón's Comedy and His Serious View of Life." In _Hispanic_ _Studies_ _in_ _Honor_ _of_ _Nicholson_ _B._ _Adams_. Chapel Hill: Univ. of North Carolina Press, 1966, pp. 179-93.

----------. "Christian and Moor in Calderón's _El príncipe_ _constante_." _Modern_ _Language_ _Review_, 53 (1958), pp. 512-20.

----------. ""El problema de la responsabilidad en la comedia de capa y espada." In _Actas_ _del_ _Segundo_ _Congreso_ _de_ _la_ _Asociación_ _Internacional_ _de Hispanistas_. Nijmegen, 1967, pp.689-94.

----------. _Introducción_ _al_ _teatro_ _religioso_ _del_ _siglo_ _de_ _oro_. Salamanca: Anaya, 1967.

----------. "Poetry and Drama in Calderón's El médico de su honra." Romanic Review, 49, No 1 (February, 1958).

----------. "The Unconscious Mind in Calderón's El pintor de su deshonra." Hispanic Review, V. 18, No. 4 (1950), pp. 285-301.

Warnke, Frank. Versions of Baroque. New Haven: Yale Univ. Press, 1972.

Watson, A.I. "El pintor de su deshonra and the Neoaristotelian Theory of Tragedy." In Critical Essays on The Theater of Calderón. Ed. Bruce Wardropper. New York: New York Univ. Press, 1965.

Wellek, Rene and Austin Warren. Theory of Literature. New York: Harcourt, Brace, and World, 1942.

Wheelwright, Philip. The Burning Fountain: A Study in The Language of Symbolism. Bloomington: Indiana Univ. Press, 1954.

----------. Metaphor and Reality. Bloomington: Indiana Univ. Press, 1962.

Whitby, William. "Calderón's El príncipe constante: Fénix's Role in the Ransom of Fernando's Body." Bulletin of the Comediantes, V. 8, No. 1 (1955), pp. 1-4.

----------. "Rosaura's Role in the Structure of La vida es sueño." Hispanic Review, 23 (1960), pp. 16-27.

Wilson, E.M. and Duncan Moir. A Literary History of Spain: The Golden Age of Drama 1492-1700. London: Benn, 1971.

---------- and W. Entwistle. "Calderón's Príncipe constante:
    Two Appreciations." Modern Language Review, 34 (1939), pp.
    pp. 207-22.

Wölfflin, Heinrich. Principles of Art History. London: G. Bell
    and Sons, 1932.

Index to Plays Cited

Index to Critics Cited